Believe In New Beginnings

Believe In New Beginnings

A Stage IV Lung Cancer Survival Journey

Susan Nix

Copyright © 2014 by Susan Nix.

ISBN:		Softcover		978-1-4990-2421-0
		eBook			978-1-4990-2942-0

All rights reserved. No part of this book may be reproduced or transmitted in any form or by any means, electronic or mechanical, including photocopying, recording, or by any information storage and retrieval system, without permission in writing from the copyright owner.

Any people depicted in stock imagery provided by Thinkstock are models, and such images are being used for illustrative purposes only.
Certain stock imagery © Thinkstock.

This book was printed in the United States of America.

Rev. date: 05/27/2014

To order additional copies of this book, contact:
Xlibris LLC
1-888-795-4274
www.Xlibris.com
Orders@Xlibris.com
619812

CONTENTS

Foreword 7
Preface 9

Chapter 1:   What a Great Life I Have, Until 11
Chapter 2:   Diagnosis and Confirmation... 16
Chapter 3:   The Journey Begins 22
Chapter 4:   How in the World Do You Talk to a Cancer Patient? 31
Chapter 5:   Taking Care of Business 33
Chapter 6:   And it Gets Tougher..39
Chapter 7:   The Ups and Downs 43
Chapter 8:   Sometimes it Gets Worse 50
Chapter 9:   And Worse 53
Chapter 10: Roller Coaster 57
Chapter 11: On the Mend? 61
Chapter 12: Getting Through the Holidays and Then the Good News 67
Chapter 13: Going Back to Work..72
Chapter 14: The First Scan After the First Scan...............................78
Chapter 15: And so it Begins 81
Chapter 16: The Long Road to Recovery 86
Chapter 17: Moving on Literally and Figuratively 90
Chapter 18: New Beginnings 94
Chapter 19: Where She is Today...98

FOREWORD

THIS BOOK IS written for the many people who have been diagnosed with any type of cancer. I've never written a book to be published before this one. You will probably find typos and some grammatical errors, but that's not the important thing. The important thing is that you find some comfort, and/or become more educated to enable you to transition through your cancer journey as comfortably as is possible.

And here's the boring stuff you can skip through if you'd like, but I need to show my gratitude for those people who were responsible for getting me to this point in my life.

First and foremost, I have to give thanks to my parents, who have always been there for me and for my siblings, but I especially feel such gratitude not only for their sacrifices during my cancer journey but also for the many trials and tribulations I caused them while I was growing up. They raised us in the Christian faith and without ever saying, they showed us that giving to others is more important than giving to ourselves. (Philippians 2: 3-5 "Do nothing out of selfish ambition or vain conceit, but in humility consider others better than yourselves. Each of you should look not only to your own interests, but also to the interests of others. Your attitude should be the same as that of Christ Jesus.") My mother has given more than five thousand hours of volunteer service to our local hospital, she has knitted dozens of baby sweater sets and donated them to the hospital gift store, crocheted numerous shawls for the cancer patients, made numerous altar linens for the church, given numerous hours of service to the church, has done community service, all without pay, since coming to this country from England, some seventy years ago. My father served in the Air Force for 22 years, has done so many things since then: he ran for County Supervisor because the encumbent had served for so many years that he was becoming a tyrant. He ran as a write-in and won against the encumbent; he helped to build, with his own hands and money the St. Nicholas Church in our hometown; to this day he continues to contribute to the community by building and refurbishing furniture for anyone who asks. And that's just the tip of the iceburg!

Thank you to my sister, Chris, for giving me such sage advice during my journey. She is a registered nurse and has always been there for me. She was taught in nursing school not to give advice to family members because she is not a doctor, but bless her heart she eventually veered away from that and gave us all the best advice whenever we called her with a problem. She told me to envision "pac-men" eating the cancer while having my chemo treatments, which I think really helped.

Thank you to my sister, Liz, for teaching me that "things" don't matter. When I would become stressed, she would say: "is it a ten"? In other words, on a scale of one to ten is that really the worst thing that could happen to you? That kept me grounded through so many difficult times in my life. I thank her for telling me to keep a journal. From the journal came this book, which I think God wanted me to write so that others can be more educated from someone else's (mine) mistakes and ignorance. And thank you for editing this book

Thank you to my brother, Michael, for always being the sane one (remember the Crisco icing on the cake at the dinner attended?), despite having to grow up with three sisters. We tormented him relentlessly when we were all young, which is probably why mom afforded him the title of "crowned prince", a title you'll later learn how he acquired.

Thanks to Robbie, a graphic designer, and my nephew, (my sister Chris's son) for doing the book cover. It was important to me to have it done by him and I am so blessed to have him do it. (BTW, if you like it, contact me and he can do some work for you!)

Thank you to the many, many people who prayed for me during my journey. God answered those prayers and because of that I am still here, and will try to spend the rest of my life finding ways to serve the Lord, with humility.

PREFACE

"**"MOM, I HAVE lung cancer."** Words no mother wants to hear. For the last several weeks, we had been hearing from Susie about various tests she has had. Finally a biopsy she had showed several abnormalities in her lungs. I can't remember what I said to her, only that we would be with her as soon as we could get a flight. When I held Susie in my arms at the airport I knew I had been right to get to her as soon as possible. She cried and I said it's all right, we are here, you will be alright now and we will take care of you."

The above paragraph is the first paragraph in the journal my mother had kept during my cancer journey. I didn't even know she had kept a journal at all until ten years after my diagnosis. My sister, Liz, had suggested she keep a journal, just as she had suggested to me.

I was diagnosed at the age of 49 with Stage IV lung cancer. And to answer your initial question, yes I smoked, from the age of 18 to 39, working up to a pack and a half each day. My oncologist told me there could be any number of reasons for the cancer (asbestos, second hand smoke since my parents smoked, or it could have been my own smoking). I think he just didn't want me to feel guilty about my own smoking and wanted me to concentrate on getting through the treatments. In my heart and gut, I know my cancer was caused because of my smoking.

When I turned 39, I quit smoking after having smoked for 21 years. While I was smoking, several people told me I should quit, but I wasn't ready to quit, so I resented them telling me to quit. Once I quit, I resolved not to be one of those people who approach folks and tell them to stamp out the cigarette because it can hurt you. Only one time did I do that very thing. On my daily walk with my golden retriever, Scottey and my other dog, Zack, through a park one day, there were two young boys who looked to be about thirteen years old. Both were tentatively smoking a cigarette. That's just all kinds of wrong. I walked past them and then decided if I could prevent these two from going through what I went through, then I had to try. I turned around and approached them and said "I used to smoke cigarettes for a long time and as a result, I got cancer and had some very painful treatments that almost killed me. You may think it looks cool to smoke, but it's harder to be cooler than that and be the one who doesn't smoke." They both just looked at me, a kind of scared look on their faces. I never saw them again so I don't know what ever happened, but I'm glad I did that.

I don't have a spouse and I live alone with my two dogs. On the one hand, it was hard because I didn't have someone to rely on/cry on, but at the same time I didn't have to worry about anyone else's worries, feelings and emotions.

I am so grateful to my sister, Liz, for suggesting I keep a journal of my cancer journey, which has led to this book. The journal did several things. It kept me focused on what was happening to my body during the cancer journey, it gave me a responsibility to do every day, it gave me something to re-read after the treatments were long gone and it gave me the impetus to write this book which I'm hoping will prepare other newly diagnosed cancer patients for what they are about to embark upon or in some way provide inspiration and hope for those diagnosed with this mysterious disease.

Probably my treatments and reactions were harsher than yours will be so please do not think you will experience the same reactions as I did. My diagnosis was Stage IV Lung Cancer. Hopefully yours is a lesser Stage and a different, more treatable and survivable cancer. It is likely yours will be easier.

I can't believe how incredibly ignorant I was about cancer; I didn't even know the difference between chemo-therapy and radiation. No two cancer patients react the same to treatments, conditions, survival rates and types of cancer, but I hope in some way this book helps you to understand the how and why of what you're going through.

Lastly, keep a positive attitude! I know it's hard sometimes, but put a note on your frig with your favorite joke. Maybe one of those in this book will become your favorite . . .

CHAPTER I

What a Great Life I Have, Until

SEPTEMBER 2003: LIFE is really good. I have a great job as a Senior Programs Manager with several project managers working for me. We have a $150 million business that is rocking and rolling. We've thoroughly pleased our customers and I've finally built a good reputation with this company.

In our business area, we repair radar components. This year, I realized we have over 1,000 components in backlog and the country is facing Desert Storm/Desert Shield. The soldiers need these radar components desperately to install into their radars in the aircrafts to fly on assigned missions. However, there is a tendency on the part of the technicians to hold on to the parts for job security, dragging out the repairs so they have something to do the next day, rather than repair them as quickly as possible and get them back to the fleet. To add to that, this facility had recently undergone a privatization (where a military facility is privatized by a non-government, commercial company). As a part of the privatization, several hundred people were laid off to trim costs. So these folks are understandably nervous about not having enough work to do to keep them employed.

We devised a plan to reduce the backlog by at least half by the end of the year and thankfully, the team embraced the plan wholeheartedly. We are so on target to the plan and I am so pleased with and grateful to all the technicians and hourly workers in Indianapolis that have been instrumental in making this happen for our customer.

A friend of mine, Cindy, invites me to a Breast Cancer Awareness Breakfast and I think "okay, whatever". We go to the breakfast and I am oblivious about the intensity and implications of cancer. I have no idea what the probabilities of survival are for each cancer. We go and I am tickled to receive a few trinket gifts.

Within three weeks of that breakfast, Cindy is diagnosed with breast cancer. How coincidental is that?

Several of us women at work had initiated a Women's Network and when we found out Cindy had been diagnosed with cancer, we got together and decided to create a basket of goodies for her, then agreed we would send her cards on a weekly basis. We started a new beginning.

I visited her several times, bringing her baskets, cards, gifts, etc. Not sure why I felt connected to her, since we didn't really work very closely together, but I did.

In January, I will start the Purdue University Krannert Executive International MBA program. During this two year program, we will go to Hungary twice, Paris twice, Netherlands twice and Purdue twice. There are three "modules" and two of the six trips will be in each module. Each of the six trips is called "In-Residency" and will be two weeks in duration. We will receive all the classroom instruction from the professors at these locations. Everything else is done electronically. How lucky am I?? My company is paying for the tuition and all international expenses, including business class travel.

November 2003: Bill, one of the project managers who worked for me is diagnosed with stomach cancer. It's not real to me because I still don't comprehend the seriousness of this terrible disease; but man, I feel really bad for him. One day, I walked into his office and he has his head in his hands. He looks really dejected and I begin to appreciate his concern. He has been told there was nothing they can do for him. But he doesn't give up. And he still comes to work every day, until his treatments prevent him from coming.

January 2004: We did it!!! Our team achieved our goal of returning half of our backlog to the fleet so they can accomplish their mission. Each month, we kept our customer apprised of our goal and progress and they were complimentary the entire way. Now finally, the year is over and we achieved our goal. Our customer came to our facility (which is unusual) to share in the celebration. All our team employees, staff, and management joined us for cake and a meeting with the customer to celebrate our success. It was one of the most satisfying times of my career.

Meanwhile, we run every day, me and the two dogs. We run about 2 miles and it always feels good. In the fall of 2003, I start feeling really tired after running only about a half a block. Strange, but not significant enough to see a doctor. My legs would immediately feel tired as if we'd already run several miles. We keep running every day and finally I think this is so wrong, I should be able to run without this intense fatigue. I call the Doctor's office and make an appointment, but can only see a nurse practitioner. She tells me it could be anything, and if it persists, I should make an appointment with the doctor. A couple months later, it still persists and I go back.

March 2004: I finally see my doctor and he takes blood and determined I had an auto-immune deficiency. He prescribed prednisone, which immediately plastered 6 pounds on me and gave me diarrhea for eight days. Later when I was diagnosed, I asked my oncologist how long the cancer had been in my body and he explained that accordingly to the growth rate, about two years. So for two years, I've been walking around with cancer, didn't know it and the only indication I had was a fatigue when running. I obsess about the fact that so many people are walking around with cancer, as I was, and don't even know it. The signs and symptoms are so subtle and some folks are so stubborn, or can't afford to see a doctor.

I'm invited to attend the annual company Leadership Forum in Waltham, Massachusetts, which is typically attended by the higher executives in the company. I am honored and baffled that I'm invited. It's quite interesting and I take copious notes of all the speeches by these Presidents, VPs and guests so that I can pass them onto my project managers. At the five course meal on the last evening (which was an absolutely amazing meal) the CEO awards are handed out. These awards are handed out only every couple of years and only to about a dozen people in the 80,000 employee company. The first award is given to some guy who did wonderful things for the company. Then the CEO starts reading the abstract on why the second person deserves the award. The more he reads, the more I'm confused, then curious, then nervous, then amazed. He's talking about me!! Then he calls my name, and I find myself on the stage getting a huge bear hug from our CEO, then holding onto this precious award. When I get back to the table my business unit president gives me the big thumbs up. After the dinner, pictures are taken of all the recipients. When I get back to my room, just who does one call?? Mom, of course. I was in such shock; all I could do was cry. I wanted my parents to be so proud of me. A major reason for receiving this award was due to leading the radar team to successfully and quickly return the customer's radar components back to them as soon as possible. And that couldn't have happened without the wonderful people who work at the Indianapolis facility.

April 2004: Both my index fingers turn very cold. I am referred to a hand surgeon and he tells me we need to figure this out or "we'll have to cut off those fingers". But we need to find the cause. No pressure there! I am so incredibly shocked at the abrupt diagnosis and can only focus on that potential surgery. I go back to work directly after that appointment, have a meeting with a peer and she immediately realizes something is wrong. I tell her what the doctor said, and then of course, start crying again. Being the compassionate person she is, (her name is Donna), and having the utmost respect for her Christian faith and Christian behavior she was so totally gentle and urged me to go home and relax.

I say utmost respect for her Christian behavior because people would talk about other people and she had this most subtle way of not engaging in the conversation, but rather disengaging without anyone really noticing. Ten years later, I'm still admiring that behavior and trying to emulate it.

I decide to get a second opinion since the first doctor was so blunt. The second surgeon tells me there is reconstructive surgery that can be performed, but first we need to find the cause. Again, the signal that we need to find the source that is causing the nerve damage. I wonder if either one of these doctors suspected it might be cancer, but couldn't say anything because they weren't the specialists who should make that diagnosis.

April 2004: I am invited to attend the Program Leadership Forum and this time I know there are awards to be handed out and that I may be a recipient; however, all the people who were nominated for this award were invited, so no one knows who the winners are. The sad thing was that the spouses of the nominees were also in attendance, so if their spouse didn't win the award, they had to sit there and watch other employees' spouses get the award. At the dinner that night, I am so blessed to be recognized again, but now with the Program Leadership award. It is a testimony to the hard work our team has accomplished over the past couple of years. I took a picture of the award and emailed it to my mom (surprise, surprise), who immediately put it on her refrigerator. It stayed there for about 10 years, until her and Dad bought a new refrigerator. Bill Cosby used to call that "refrigerator art", art that your children proudly create, and then bring home to their parents for displaying on the refrigerator.

COMIC RELIEF:

The FBI had an opening for an assassin. After all of the background checks, interviews and testing were done there were three finalists, two men and a woman.

For the final test, the FBI agents took one of the men to a large metal door and handed him a gun. "We must know that you will follow your instructions, no matter what the circumstances. Inside of this room you will find your wife sitting in a chair, Kill her!!!"

The man said, "You can't be serious. I could never shoot my wife." The agent said, "Then you're not the right man for this job."

The second man was given the same instructions. He took the gun and went into the room. All was quiet for about five minutes, Then the man come out with tears in his eyes. "I tried, but I can't kill my wife." The agent said, "You don't have what it takes. Take your wife and go home".

Finally, it was the woman's turn. She was given the same instructions, to kill her husband. She took the gun and went into the room. Shots were heard. One shot after another. They heard screaming, crashing and banging on the walls. After a few minutes, all was quiet. The door opened slowly and there stood the woman. She wiped the sweat from her brow, and said, "This gun is loaded with blanks. I had to beat him to death with the chair."

CHAPTER 2

Diagnosis and Confirmation

MAY 2004: BACK to the doc because I'm still fatigued when running, and have a feeling that there is something in my throat that is blocking my breathing and also my index fingers are still so cold. The doctor prescribes an esophogram and thyroid uptake, but both come back normal. I don't recommend either of these tests if you want to maintain a comfortable, relaxing day. Since those tests didn't provide any answers, they take an x-ray of my throat. Seems like that would have been an easier, less expensive and less invasive testing, but this is just another instance where I didn't question what I was directed to do.

June 2004: The doctor also schedules an angiogram on my right hand which confirms damaged vessels in the index, third and fifth fingers. But the test still does not provide a diagnosis on the cause. After the surgery, the nurse tells me to be very careful not to tear the incision in my groin from the angiogram and cause any bleeding because I could bleed out very easily. They had placed a huge bandage on the incision. When I get home, I'm very careful to walk slowly, sit down and get up slowly and really just baby myself. The next day I take off the bandage to take a shower and just about died laughing. The incision is only about a third of an inch long! In my mind I had imagined a huge, deep incision with stitches and everything! While the bleeding scare was real, I probably overdid the precaution.

Fast forward to 2014, I have been asked by an oncologist to bring my golden retriever to a Cancer Support Group session to help the patients relax. I hear a patient's wife ask about neuropathy and my ears perk up because she is talking about nerve damage and I start thinking about my poor Reynaud's fingers and the fact that my legs started feeling tired with exercise, which is unusual. When I get home, I do research and learn it is nerve damage caused by cancer!!! It can also be caused by chemo-therapy, so double whammy! It causes nerve damage (to my fingers) and causes weakness (to my legs causing tiredness in running). To be more exact, it is called peripheral neuropathy: peripheral (beyond brain and spinal cord), neuro (related to nerves), pathy (disease). It is common in persons greater than 55 years of age. Whoo-hoo, ain't it great to be old!

June 2004: Now I get a call from my Primary Care Physician and I'm told to come back to his office and have a Cat Scan (CT) of my chest. Unbeknownst to me (you'll see this is a recurring theme throughout this book, unbeknownst to me because I didn't have the knowledge/brainpower/intelligence to ask questions at the time something was being explained to me), from the throat x-ray, they saw the tumor in my chest.

For the CT, you have to fast and then drink a lot of liquid so your organs are amplified. A couple of days after the CT, the doctor's office calls and asks me to come in about 6:00 pm with "someone important in my life". Again, I ignorantly think, "that's strange, the office is closed by 6:00 pm, how nice of him to keep it open for me, he must be really busy". My son, daughter-in-law and granddaughter (6 months old) come with me and I am told there is a tumor in my chest. I'm thinking "Ok, no big deal, I'll deal with this and have it cut out". And I'm in denial. He refers me to a pulmonologist for a consult. What the heck does a pulmonologist do? Turns out he/she is a lung specialist. I'm still so ignorant and of course the doctors don't spend a lot of time explaining anything at this point because the degree of seriousness hasn't yet been determined. Actually, in retrospect, I don't think my son and daughter-in-law thought this was anything serious to deal with either.

July 2004: The most incredible day of my life so far. I have never seen so many specialists in one day in my entire life. First was a rheumatologist for which I had an appointment to discuss the coldness in my fingers. She did an evaluation on me and said there is something wrong with my hands (really?) and we'll try different meds to correct it. She states that I have "Reynaud's", a phenomenon that prevents circulation in the extremities. She prescribes cozaar, which over time, she increases the dosage to the maximum available, none of which has any effect on the lack of sensation in my fingers.

After that, I have an appointment with an oncologist, Dr. Keith Logie at the Central Indiana Cancer Center (CICC), who states the problem indicated by the CT scan might be lymphoma or something else, then he reviews the films and shows me some "areas that shouldn't be there" and then points out the tumor. It looked like a little amoeba. I now know he is trying to deal the blow slowly. He refers me to the pulmonologist (aka Lung Specialist). I leave Dr. Logie's office and am sent directly to the Lung Specialist who looks at my ex-rays and says it probably isn't good. I was distracted just a little because he was so darned good looking! None of this is sounding highly medical at this point. However, this is now becoming kind of serious. There are just too many people giving me bad news.

After the appointment with the Lung Specialist, I am scheduled to again meet with Dr. Logie. He asks if I want confirmation of the diagnosis from the Lung Specialist. And I ask what that would entail. He explains we could do a mediastinoscopy, which is a procedure where they will anesthetize me, place an incision on my throat and with a scope take several samples in my chest. I answer yes, let's do it.

I'm told to go to the clinic and have some blood drawn. They draw 17 vials of blood. Without a doubt, that's the most blood I've ever had drawn in my life. I'm only 5 feet tall and 110 pounds. How much of my blood did I just lose? Little did I know how many other new things I would soon have to experience.

My son, Ashley, is in the United States Marine Corps and is now stationed in Afghanistan for 6 months. The mediastinoscopy is performed and my daughter in law, Amy, who is living with me, takes me there and drives me home. My granddaughter is with her so it's kind of inconvenient for her. As I'm coming out of the anesthesia, the doctor tells Amy all five findings are "abnormal". So now I have a tumor and five abnormal findings. I don't know what the abnormal findings mean. Is that more tumors, spots of something or what? Okay, no problem we'll deal with it. I'm so naïve. And I'm in denial.

I am still too out of it from the anesthesia to process this information. And they gave me too much anesthesia from the mediastinoscopy so Amy has to pull over so I can vomit on the way home. How gross. We get home and I'm exhausted but I have folks scheduled to come in and install speakers in the house that day so I would have TV and music in the family/dining/kitchen room. I'm embarrassed to look so out of it and am so tired; I have to lie on the couch while they finish their work. Little did I know that was just the beginning of looking so abnormal. See how I'm still not processing the seriousness?

The next morning when I woke up, I have a golf ball size lump in my throat from the procedure yesterday and it lasts about 3-4 days. If someone explained that that would be the result of the surgery, I certainly don't remember that. I just keep looking more and more beautiful. Not!

July 2004: This is absolutely the worst day of my life. My chemo oncologist has the results from the mediastinoscopy and tells me I have lung cancer. He's so sorry and wishes it was lymphoma as he had originally speculated. Thank goodness, my good friend, Mike, offered to come with me to hear this news. He must have known the results wouldn't be good long before I did. I cry and cry, still not really appreciating the gravity and severity of the situation and the very difficult treatment and reactions I am about to face. Certainly, I have no clue about how the treatments would change my life forever. At this time, my doctor tells me it is Stage IIIB, Lung Cancer, Non-Small Cell Carcinoma. I later learn it was really Stage IV all along because it had metastasized (spread) to a lump in my throat.

One of my college courses was "Ethical Options in Medicine". Absolutely nothing to do with my business degree, but I thought it would be an interesting elective course to take, and it was. In this class I learned that Elisabeth Kubler Ross defined the five stages of death and dying. The idea being that it is important to allow the patient to experience each stage and progress to the next stage.

1. *Denial and isolation: a stage where you can't accept what you're being told. You think, not me; no one in my family has this problem. (So you can probably see by now that I have clearly been in this stage.)*
2. *Anger: The Why me? Stage. I haven't done anything to deserve this.*
3. *Bargaining: Ok, I'll be a better Christian, I won't cuss anymore, and I'll do anything, just make this go away.*
4. *Depression: I don't like this, I don't want this, I'm very sad.*
5. *Acceptance: Allows the patient to accept the fate, no matter how severe the prognosis, even death.*

They say the average person retains about 20% of what they learn during their college courses, so I find it quite coincidental and fortuitous that retaining this information about death and dying is something I would retain and that it had nothing to do with my pursuit of a business degree and everything to do with my cancer journey!

Stage IV Non-Small Cell Lung Cancer defines a lung tumor of any size that has spread (metastasized) to another region of the body, to another part of the lungs, or is accompanied by a malignant pleural effusion. A pleural effusion is an abnormal amount of fluid between the tissues that line the lungs. If that is cancerous, it is considered malignant; therefore, malignant pleural effusion. Also, non-small cell cancer is impervious to chemo-therapy. I know this now because I did research after all my treatments were complete and I am so surprised and grateful that indeed my treatments were able to eradicate the cancer. I had no idea what the doctor was talking about at the time. I was later to learn my cancer had spread throughout my lungs and had also spread to my throat so I was indeed Stage IV, but I did not have the pleural effusion. So that's what the five abnormal findings were . . . lymph nodes that contained cancer.

I mention to my doctor that yesterday at work I started seeing scintillating sparks or lights. He immediately schedules an MRI on the brain. An MRI to the brain requires you to be placed on a horizontal table and they clasp a "cage" over onto your head. If you're lucky, they will hand you a head phone so you can listen to music during the test. Say yes, because the test consists of several consecutive very loud sounds. The music barely drowns out the loud sounds. Some people with claustrophia may be unable to manage this test.

The doctor states "that would change the entire picture". That worries me immediately because I instinctively knew chemo-therapy or radiation to the brain can be dangerous. The scan is done the same morning. Mike and I go to lunch while we wait for the results of the MRI. The doctor calls me while we're eating and I just start boo-hooing. Luckily there is nothing wrong with my brain. This is such an emotional roller coaster. So, I never find out what caused those scintillating sparks that day and thankfully they never recurred.

No one in my immediate family, to my knowledge, has ever had cancer. None of us have ever had to deal with anything catastrophic like this.

Coincidentally, however, my cousin Tim has also been diagnosed with cancer. He died while I was going through my treatments, but I don't learn this until later. My parents, as well as others, graciously protected me from the bad news of others going through cancer treatments.

After lunch, Mike and I go back to my house and he calls my boss to give him the slap happy news of my cancer diagnosis. I don't hear the conversation because Mike steps outside to talk. Now, this guy, my boss, is a guy who has tormented me relentlessly since I came to Indiana. Either he hates females in the workplace or resents that I was transferred from California to Indiana while the company was laying-off Indiana workers due to the privatization. He's the kind of boss who embarrasses you in front of your peers. There were times when I drove home crying from the harassment. My plan of survival was that I would kill him with happiness, never let him see me suffer, always respond happily. And I worked my butt off. Eventually, thankfully, I earned his respect and I believe he is the one who later nominated me for the CEO and Program Leadership awards.

For the past several months, I have been keeping my folks informed of my various ailments and telling them something isn't right and I'm having tests. No conclusive results yet, but I'll let them know as soon as I hear something. By now, they, and I know it's not the flu or a cold, but something a little more serious that we'll have to deal with.

Once I get the results, I call my parents and tell them "now would be a good time to come; I have lung cancer". Of course they immediately jump on a plane and come, even though my mom has a fear of heights and can't easily fly. She has to take drugs to make the trip. They must have already had their bags packed, immediately made the flight arrangements, made arrangements for my sister to take care of the house, mail, etc. I found out later that my mom refused to go anywhere that day until I called. You know, your child will always be your child. I am 49 years old and my parents still came running right away. My son is 22 years old and he will always be my child and my baby. If anything like this ever happened to him, I'd be there in a second.

My parents arrive at the airport the next day and as soon as I see my mom we hug each other tightly and I start crying. I felt so relieved and comforted. She said "it's all right, we're here now and we'll take care of you". Isn't it funny, I'm still my momma's baby? Well, at least one of them, she also has two other daughters and a spoiled son. My brother has been so spoiled that my mom's email address is cpmum, which stands for Crowned Prince Mum; crowned prince for the spoiled brother and Mum because she is British.

I receive a phone call from a woman who says a mutual friend of ours had told her I had been diagnosed with cancer and she was selling an herbal product. She states it would be helpful to me during my treatment program. At first I was offended that she would take advantage of my situation in order for her to make money and I tell her I'll call her if I'm interested. Much later, I would come to understand she never discussed money and probably believed her product would truly help me in some way. Maybe I should have given her product a chance, but I didn't know at the time how difficult my treatments were to become. Then I never gave her another thought. So my advice is to never throw away any offers of kindness/healing. And, unfortunately, I never learned who the mutual friend was that referred her to me, so I could thank him or her.

COMIC RELIEF:

An atheist professor was teaching a college class and he told the class that he was going to prove that there is no God. He said, "God, if you are real, then knock me off this platform. I'll give you 15 minutes!" Ten minutes went by. He kept taunting God, saying, "Here I am, God. I'm still waiting." He got down to the last couple of minutes and a Marine, newly registered in the class, walked up to the professor, hit him full force in the face, and sent him flying from the platform. The professor struggled to stand up, was obviously shaken and yelled, "What's the matter with you? Why did you do that?" The Marine replied, "God was busy, He sent me."

CHAPTER 3

The Journey Begins

A COUPLE OF weeks later, I meet with my chemo-therapy oncologist, Dr. Keith Logie and my radiation oncologist, Dr. Michael Hardacre. They tell me the chemo will be every week for six months. My lucky day for chemo turned out to be every Thursday. The radiation will be for 33 days every day except Saturday and Sunday, concurrent with the chemo. My radiation oncologist spends about two hours explaining that I have "non-small cell cancer called adenocarcinoma, poorly differentiated". He took great lengths to explain the cancer, how the stages are determined, etc. I am Stage IIIB out of 4 stages. Treatment will be a combination of radiation and chemotherapy. Surgery is out of the question, too dangerous at this point. Why didn't I ask "why too dangerous"? I later learn that surgery to remove the tumor wouldn't have done any good because the cancer had spread to my lymph nodes. And it is more important at this point to start the treatments, than to have useless surgery and then wait for recovery before beginning treatments. He says "we're going to have to hit you very hard with the treatments in order to make an impact". Again, no clue what that really means. Are you starting to detect a trend here (not asking what are you talking about)?? He says "the treatments will make you very tired and that is to be expected". I'm told my survival rate is about 15% after five years. I go home and check WebMD, which states survival is about 2% for Stage IV. (What is this by now, the third suggested survival rate by another source. Since there was a tumor in my throat, it had metastasized, making it stage IV. I'm sure they told me Stage IIIB to keep my morale up as high as possible. Being told you have the worst stage would probably put most people into a severe depression and tail spin.

The following is from the National Cancer Institute's Website on Cancer Staging:

Key Points:

- *Staging describes the extent or severity of a person's cancer. Knowing the stage of disease helps the doctor plan treatment and estimate the person's prognosis.*
- *Staging systems for cancer have evolved over time and continue to change as scientists learn more about cancer.*
- *The TNM staging system is based on the size and/or extent (reach) of the primary tumor (T), whether cancer cells have spread to nearby (regional) lymph nodes (N), and whether metastasis (M), or the spread of the cancer to other parts of the body, has occurred.*
- *Physical exams, imaging procedures, laboratory tests, pathology reports, and surgical reports provide information to determine the stage of a cancer.*

1. *What is staging?*

Staging describes the severity of a person's cancer based on the size and/or extent (reach) of the original (primary) tumor and whether or not cancer has spread in the body. Staging is important for several reasons:

- *Staging helps the doctor plan the appropriate treatment.*
- *Cancer stage can be used in estimating a person's prognosis.*
- *Knowing the stage of cancer is important in identifying clinical trials that may be a suitable treatment option for a patient.*
- *Staging helps health care providers and researchers exchange information about patients; it also gives them a common terminology for evaluating the results of clinical trials and comparing the results of different trials.*

Staging is based on knowledge of the way cancer progresses. Cancer cells grow and divide without control or order, and they do not die when they should. As a result, they often form a mass of tissue called a tumor. As a tumor grows, it can invade nearby tissues and organs. Cancer cells can also break away from a tumor and enter the bloodstream or the lymphatic system. By moving through the bloodstream or lymphatic system, cancer cells can spread from the primary site to lymph nodes or to other organs, where they may form new tumors. The spread of cancer is called metastasis.

2. **What are the common elements of staging systems?**

Staging systems for cancer have evolved over time. They continue to change as scientists learn more about cancer. Some staging systems cover many types of cancer; others focus on a particular type. The common elements considered in most staging systems are as follows:

- Site of the primary tumor and the cell type (e.g., adenocarcinoma, squamous cell carcinoma)
- Tumor size and/or extent (reach)
- Regional lymph node involvement (the spread of cancer to nearby lymph nodes)
- Number of tumors (the primary tumor and the presence of metastatic tumors, or metastases)
- Tumor grade* (how closely the cancer cells and tissue resemble normal cells and tissue)

*More information can be found in the NCI fact sheet Tumor Grade.

3. **What is the TNM system?**

The TNM system is one of the most widely used cancer staging systems. This system has been accepted by the Union for International Cancer Control (UICC) and the American Joint Committee on Cancer (AJCC). Most medical facilities use the TNM system as their main method for cancer reporting.

The TNM system is based on the size and/or extent (reach) of the primary tumor (**T**), the amount of spread to nearby lymph nodes (**N**), and the presence of metastasis (**M**) or secondary tumors formed by the spread of cancer cells to other parts of the body. A number is added to each letter to indicate the size and/or extent of the primary tumor and the degree of cancer spread.

Primary Tumor (T)
TX: Primary tumor cannot be evaluated
T0: No evidence of primary tumor
Tis: Carcinoma in situ (CIS; abnormal cells are present but have not spread to neighboring tissue; although not cancer, CIS may become cancer and is sometimes called preinvasive cancer)
T1, T2, T3, T4: Size and/or extent of the primary tumor

Regional Lymph Nodes (N)
NX: Regional lymph nodes cannot be evaluated
N0: No regional lymph node involvement

N1, N2, N3: *Degree of regional lymph node involvement (number and location of lymph nodes)*

Distant Metastasis (M)
MX: *Distant metastasis cannot be evaluated*
M0: *No distant metastasis*
M1: *Distant metastasis is present*

For example, breast cancer classified as T3 N2 M0 refers to a large tumor that has spread outside the breast to nearby lymph nodes but not to other parts of the body. Prostate cancer T2 N0 M0 means that the tumor is located only in the prostate and has not spread to the lymph nodes or any other part of the body.

For many cancers, TNM combinations correspond to one of five stages. Criteria for stages differ for different types of cancer. For example, bladder cancer T3 N0 M0 is stage III, whereas colon cancer T3 N0 M0 is stage II.

Stage	Definition
Stage 0	Carcinoma in situ
Stage I, Stage II, and Stage III	Higher numbers indicate more extensive disease: Larger tumor size and/or spread of the cancer beyond the organ in which it first developed to nearby lymph nodes and/or tissues or organs adjacent to the location of the primary tumor
Stage IV	The cancer has spread to distant tissues or organs

Question 6 describes sources of additional information about staging for specific types of cancer.

4. Are all cancers staged with TNM classifications?

Most types of cancer have TNM designations, but some do not. For example, cancers of the brain and spinal cord are staged according to their cell type and grade. Different staging systems are also used for many cancers of the blood or bone marrow, such as lymphomas. The Ann Arbor staging classification is commonly used to stage lymphomas and has been adopted by both the AJCC and the UICC. However, other cancers of the blood or bone marrow, including most types of leukemia, do not have a clear-cut staging system. Another staging system, developed by the International Federation of Gynecology and Obstetrics (FIGO), is used to stage cancers of the cervix, uterus, ovary, vagina, and vulva. This system is also based on TNM information. Additionally, most childhood cancers are staged using either the TNM system or the staging criteria of the Children's Oncology Group (COG), which conducts pediatric clinical trials; however, other staging systems may be used for some childhood cancers.

Many cancer registries, such as those supported by NCI's Surveillance, Epidemiology, and End Results (SEER) Program, use "summary staging." This system is used for all types of cancer. It groups cancer cases into five main categories:

o **In situ**: Abnormal cells are present only in the layer of cells in which they developed
o **Localized**: Cancer is limited to the organ in which it began, without evidence of spread
o **Regional**: Cancer has spread beyond the primary site to nearby lymph nodes or tissues and organs
o **Distant**: Cancer has spread from the primary site to distant tissues or organs or to distant lymph nodes
o **Unknown**: There is not enough information to determine the stage

5. *What types of tests are used to determine stage?*

The types of tests used for staging depend on the type of cancer. Tests include the following:

o **Physical exams** are used to gather information about the cancer. The doctor examines the body by looking, feeling, and listening for anything unusual. The physical exam may show the location and size of the tumor(s) and the spread of the cancer to the lymph nodes and/or to other tissues and organs.
o **Imaging studies** produce pictures of areas inside the body. These studies are important tools in determining stage. Procedures such as x-rays, computed tomography (CT) scans, magnetic resonance imaging (MRI) scans, and positron emission tomography (PET) scans can show the location of the cancer, the size of the tumor, and whether the cancer has spread.
o **Laboratory tests** are studies of blood, urine, other fluids, and tissues taken from the body. For example, tests for liver function and tumor markers (substances sometimes found in increased amounts if cancer is present) can provide information about the cancer.
o **Pathology reports** may include information about the size of the tumor, the growth of the tumor into other tissues and organs, the type of cancer cells, and the grade of the tumor. A biopsy may be performed to provide information for the pathology report. Cytology reports also describe findings from the examination of cells in body fluids.

o   ***Surgical reports*** *tell what is found during surgery. These reports describe the size and appearance of the tumor and often include observations about lymph nodes and nearby organs.*

6. *How can a patient find more information about staging?*

The doctor most familiar with a patient's situation is in the best position to provide staging information for that person. For background information, PDQ®, NCI's comprehensive cancer information database, contains cancer treatment summaries that describe the staging of adult and childhood cancers.

In retrospect, I think my doctors kind of spoon fed me how hard the treatments would really be or maybe I just didn't want to believe the possibility of this being terminal. Had I known in the beginning what I would be experiencing, I probably wouldn't have had the stamina to go on. They told me to take care of myself and to eat properly, but I don't think I really comprehended the magnitude of the situation and the importance of eating healthy foods, instead of the comfort foods that I tried to get down my throat.

Being so independent for so long, my pragmatic thought process throughout this was to get things in order. I secure a lawyer who draws up my will. I secure my plot at Evergreen Conference Center Oakhurst (ECCO), which is a beautiful Christian area in northern California which, among other things, has small plots you can purchase where your remains can be placed with a plaque engraved with your name and then placed on top of the plot. It is very well done, in an area that is just so peaceful and calming. In fact, if there was music playing, you might think you were in heaven.

What type of person are you? Procrastinator, organizer, protector, etc.? How will you react to getting things in order, if need be?

One of the things, besides prayers, that I am convinced saved my life was a positive attitude. There came a time when I did get very depressed, but for the most part, my spirits were pretty darned good.

The clinic then did a simulation radiation treatment, marking my chest with permanent markers to align the lasers. My first real treatment is scheduled for July 29. How strange to have all these permanent marks all over my chest. Good thing I don't have a husband to see all that ugliness. I remember worrying about taking a shower and washing off the marks, but no problem, the clinic had an abundance of markers and would happily re-mark me each time. After 2-3 weeks, they had the lasers lined up perfectly and no longer needed to draw pretty pictures all over my body.

Again, I am so grateful to my sister who suggested I keep a journal. So much has happened to me during my cancer treatments that I did not later recall. And you do get "chemo brain", an affliction that prevents you from remembering a lot of things even after the completion of the treatments.

By now, my friend Bill has had stomach surgery to remove as much of the tumor as possible, but he still has terminal cancer. He has done research into Bethesda Hospital where stem cell transplants are proving successful. He lines up his sister to donate stem cells and arranges his induction into the program.

My friend, Cindy, has had a number of CT/Pet scans and the last one showed her cancer has spread to her liver, back and stomach so she has begun a stronger regimen of chemo-therapy.

My best friend in California, Mary, starts calling me every Friday to check up on me. The word has gotten around with my California friends about my situation. One of my previous bosses calls me to relay his throat cancer journey, which made me feel very sad as they had to remove a part of his throat.

July 21 (my son's birthday):

The doctor orders a CT scan on my abdomen to determine if cancer has spread to my tummy, which he said was fairly common. The results came back normal-it has not spread. We went up to the head with the MRI and down to the tummy with the CT and now we know we're only dealing with cancer in the lungs and throat.

July 22: This is my first chemo-therapy treatment and I am placed in a private room and know this is a one-time occurrence because I see many other patients receiving chemo in a large community room. The nurse starts the chemo with an IV in my arm and it takes about 6 hours. I feel fine afterward, but a little full/bulky/fat. My folks don't really seem to spend much time reading the materials and watching the video the staff had provided. Maybe they were in the "denial" stage. So my suggestion to you is to be aware of what type of background your family/support system has had. Are they open and honest, quiet and non-talkative, or just complacent? Knowing this you may be better prepared to deal with the reactions and how to deal with them. I think my folks might have been over-whelmed with the reality of all this (as I was) and the seriousness of its impact. Eventually, my mom really comes to appreciate all the information that was provided to us because of the severity of my reactions to the treatments.

My boss decides I can no longer do my job, presumably because he knows better than I what I am about to face, that it will be difficult, will prevent me front doing a good job and partly because he wants to protect the business and make sure it doesn't falter. He replaces me with my second in command, so now, in essence, I no longer have a job except to turn over my duties to this guy. And seriously, they don't give me any duties or responsibilities to conduct each day when I come in, but they don't tell me I can't come in.

Having been single for the past twenty years, I've learned to deal with the ups and downs that life has dealt. But this has been an incredible journey and everything has recently been coming so quickly; the tests, the many doctor appointments, the diagnosis, the treatment plan. I soon feel so helpless and useless going to work each day and knowing nothing is expected of me. I've gone from being a Senior Programs Manager, managing a $150 million/year business to coming in every day, trying to find something to do.

That night we go to dinner at Ruth Chris and I decide not to have wine. Bummer. There is so much liquid in my body from the treatment today that my extremities are so swollen, I can hardly get into my shoes. Then I realize it is probably a result of non-invasive fluids and not so much chemo. Darn it, I could have had the wine.

I began to wonder how oncologists know how much chemo to administer? What if too much is too much or not enough? Everyone is different, every cancer is different. The research I found indicated that with Stage IV, Lung Cancer, the oncologist should find the dose that controls the cancer and affords the patient with the greatest quality of life and treatment that can be given off and on for the rest of the patient's life. I am so grateful to my chemo and radiation oncologists for taking a different tactic. They provided me with the most aggressive treatments of chemo and radiation, not to prolong my life, but to eradicate the cancer altogether. I come to learn many years later, that although I keep celebrating my cancer-freeness, there are many, many cancer survivors whose cancer recurs in a different part of their bodies, sometimes many years later.

Each week, the routine will be to have my blood checked, weight, blood pressure and temperature taken first. Then I have an appointment with my oncologist to discuss the day's plan and so I quickly learn to prepare a list of questions to ask. After all that, I go home and research the answers and begin preparing the list of questions for the next week. So back to the weekly appointment, I go into the chemo lounge and pick a chair that will be my home for the next six hours. It doesn't really matter which one, but I usually try to pick chairs away from others since I don't know what to expect and don't want to bother other people. Then, eventually, I will be taken from the chemo lounge to the radiation chamber for that treatment, dragging my IV pole with me. On the days I don't have chemo, I come in and go straight to the radiation chamber.

July 23: Went to work today and felt no different than before the treatment.

COMIC RELIEF:

I urgently needed a few days off work, but I knew the Boss would not allow me to take a leave. I thought that maybe if I acted "CRAZY" then he would tell me to take a few days off. So I hung upside down on the ceiling and made funny noises. My co-worker asked me what I was doing. I told her that I was pretending to be a light bulb so that the Boss would think I was "CRAZY" and give me a few days off. A few minutes later the Boss came into the office and asked "What are you doing?" I told him I was a light bulb. He said "You are clearly stressed out. Go home and recuperate for a couple of days". I Jumped down and walked out of the office. When my co-worker followed me, the Boss asked her ". . . And where do you think you're going?" She said, "I'm going home too, I can't work in the dark.

CHAPTER 4

How in the World Do You Talk to a Cancer Patient?

JULY 26: WENT to work (Monday) and it was one of the most depressing days since this all began. I spoke with Erika, who is the Director of the Master's program and told her that due to the diagnosis and treatments, I'd miss the two In-Residencies in the final module. Since I will have to miss both In-Residencies in this module, we agreed it would be better if I deferred completing the program until next year.

Then my boss comes in and asks what I'm doing at work? Duh! I think he's uncomfortable with me at work. Wait until my hair falls out and there is physical evidence of the disease! Maybe he's trying to get me to stay home, so they don't have to pay me.

Then one of the guys who works for me comes into my office and tells me people are uncertain about how to approach me, what to say. I didn't realize others would be as uncomfortable as I am. I think it's the uncertainty, the not knowing if I'm going to survive or not. Or they just don't know what to say, not knowing how I am feeling. And I am reminded of the day I saw Bill in his office with his head in his hands and I didn't know what to say to him to comfort him. So far, Bill and Cindy had been diagnosed with cancer, left work and were not expected to return to work. I guess I'm just stubborn.

It really surprised me to learn that others were as uncomfortable as me. It's the ignorance of the disease, what the patient is going through and the helplessness of not being able to help make it better. And it's also the guilt that it's you and not me.

And I am reminded of how ignorant I was when Bill and Cindy were diagnosed and how I didn't know what to say to them.

Probably the best thing you can say to a cancer patient is "I'm here for you" instead of "I know how you feel" because every cancer patient feels differently and no one really knows how they feel. Heck, they feel differently almost every single day!

If you have any good jokes, that can help depending upon which of Kubler Ross's defined stages the patient is in (anger, denial, bargaining, etc.). Although you might want to wait until the person gets to the acceptance stage.

Just listening is good. I wanted to talk, but usually it was about what was happening to me and my body and about those things I didn't understand.

Offer to help: to go to the grocery store for them, or take them to the grocery store, take them to church, take them out to lunch and/or a movie. These outings will get them out of the house focusing on something other than their predicament and will also encourage conversations. If you can arrange it once in a while, take them to their treatment session and stay there with them. Play cards with them, watch a movie, pray. It gets really lonely there.

Later when I move back to my home town of Atwater, I take my dog, Scottey to the hospital and Cancer Center as a Pet Therapy dog to lighten the days of the patients. You should see the faces light up when I walk into the patients' rooms and chemo lounge with him. It is so therapeutic to pet a dog when you're stuck in the hospital for days or in the chemo chair for hours on end and it also breaks up the monotony. I wish I had that pleasure when I was having treatments and hospitalized during my journey.

COMIC RELIEF:

Reaching the end of a job interview, the human resources person asked a young architect fresh out of a top technical university what kind of a salary he was looking for.

He replied: "In the neighborhood of $140,000 a year, depending on the benefits package."

"Well, what would you say to a package of 5 weeks' vacation, 14 paid holidays, full medical and dental, company matching retirement fund to 50% of salary, and a company car leased every 2 years . . . say, a red Corvette?"

"Wow! Are you kidding?"

"Yeah, but you started it."

CHAPTER 5

Taking Care of Business

JULY 27: I spend the rest of the day at work trying to find things to do, although not very successfully. I've gone from having a very responsible, high pressure job to a fake job trying to look busy and feel useful.

To top everything off, I am feeling disoriented and achy-painy all day. Goodness, I've only had four chemo treatments and already I'm feeling the effects. Needless to say, I cried when I got home and my folks were there to console me.

And so begins the fourth stage of Elisabeth Kubler Ross's Five Stages of Death and Dying: Depression. I completely skipped the second stage of Anger. Not sure why that happened. Perhaps not everyone goes completely through all five stages.

July 27: I had a PET scan and it took about 1 ½ hours. I couldn't eat after midnight the night before so I was really hungry. After the scan, I had a Big Mac and some fries, comfort food. My appetite left about 2-3 weeks ago and I'm back to my pre-prednisone weight.

Mom and I went to a wig place today. They had told me the hair will start falling out after about four weeks of chemo-therapy. Prior to this, I didn't know whether it was the chemo or radiation that made one's hair fall out. Now I know it's the chemo. I bought a synthetic wig and some hats. The hats came in handy because my head would get cold and of course you lose a lot of body heat through your head. The wig looks fake and I'm tempted to go without it.

Someone had recommended this place to me and they were right on. The owner was so very kind and compassionate. She would show me a couple of wigs, then walk away to let me try them on. I could tell she had done this before and was letting me have my space to put the wig on and look in the mirror and realize there's a different person looking back at me. I tried very hard not to cry. I think I'll call a few of the other places and check on human hair wigs

July 28: Went to work today and felt pretty darned good.

Driving home from work I see a billboard advertising a 1.25% mortgage rate and I'm thinking whoo-hoo, I can save money on my fixed-price mortgage which was around 5.25%. Never, ever, consider signing any legal documents while undergoing chemo-therapy and taking associated medications. It turns out this scam was for an adjustable rate which gets progressively higher each month until it can reach a maximum of 19%. During the signing, the guy just kept turning the pages and having me sign each page, not really explaining the serious constraints of the contract. And GUESS WHAT? I didn't ask any questions! Fortunately, after all my treatments and the sale of this home, I was able to get out from under this fiasco. Lesson learned, you don't have the appropriate reasoning ability to make life changing, significant financial decisions.

July 29: Second round of chemo and it takes six hours and so far I feel pretty good. The Benadryl knocked me out for an hour. I take my Walkman (didn't have a smart phone at the time), a book to read and a couple of snacks, although I never eat them. How funny, it is just my human instinct to have food around if I'm away from home for that long. While having chemo, they would then disconnect me from the chemo and take me over for the first radiation treatment, IV pole and all. It takes about an hour to get me aligned with the lasers. They radiate the front, then I roll over and they radiate the back. This is quite an ordeal. Once completely aligned, it should only take about 15 minutes each time.

My brother, (remember him, the spoiled one?), whose actual name is Michael, is a construction company vice president and he told me of a cancer radiation building his company had built in which the walls were several feet thick, and the doors the same thickness. It's a rather humbling, scary feeling to lie on that table knowing the radiation is so bad for you that other people have to be protected behind such thick walls.

My radiation oncologist went over the results of the PET scan from two days ago. The cancer hasn't spread into the abdomen, but the lymph nodes in my throat are cancerous, surprisingly the one of the left more than the one of the right. I didn't even know there were two. I'm sure they told me, but somehow it didn't register. The right node is where I first discovered the lump last fall and the fullness in my throat when I ran. So this explains why I eventually have so much trouble eating after all the radiation: because they had to radiate both sides of my throat and neck.

I call five more wig places today trying to find human hair wigs. Only talked to one lady and she didn't think they would be available until September. So I may have to wear the synthetic one until then. Fast forward to 2011, I'm in a Kiwanis meeting and the speaker for that meeting is the Chairperson for the 2012 Relay for Life event. She explains that the organization can provide wigs for cancer patients at no cost. So why didn't anyone tell me that before and why didn't I know to ask around??

While having treatment today, I meet a sweet lady named Angie. She was there for her second go-round of breast cancer treatment. She's the third person I've talked with at length who has said their cancer has recurred. I can't help but wonder how many rounds of cancer recurrence I will encounter.

Sometime around now, Mom decides to read the brochure from the cancer clinic and understands what I need to do to survive (always use new makeup, no sun exposure, eat healthy, be careful about temperatures, be careful about chills and shakes, careful about ports, etc.) and she becomes so much more conscientious and helpful about the requirements to keep me compliant with the cautions. All these precautions are to ensure I don't develop any infection which would seriously impact future treatments and recovery since my immune system is compromised from all the treatments which destroy all the red and white blood cells,. Unfortunately, I eventually do end up being careless and contract a blood infection, which set me back a couple of times.

I'm told I will need several needle pricks each week for the blood tests and the chemo treatment and I should consider installing a port so I decide that's a good thing. The needles have been hurting quite a bit. A port is, at least for me, a circular device installed just under the skin in the chest, with a tube that extends into the veins. This procedure will protect the veins in my arms and/or hands from collapsing from all the needle pricks week after week. I get scheduled for out-patient surgery for a port installation and my folks take me to the hospital. My surgeon introduces himself to me and I think "this guy is a young, young man, younger than me". I say something like "you look very young, are you quite able to perform this surgery?" He just smiled as if he'd heard that a million times. I'm put under sedation and the port is installed. I come home and discover how incredibly difficult it is that night to move or get up to go potty. Maybe I'm just being a wuss.

They didn't tell me it would be this hard. It takes several days before I can get back to normal from the port installation. And then every time I get pricked for the weekly blood test or the chemo, it still hurts just as much to puncture the skin into the port as it did to prick a new vein in the arm. But on the positive side, the port is saving my veins from collapsing from so many pricks (needles, not guys).

Then a couple of days later I call Dubbie (my hair stylist) and tell her I have purchased a wig and need it cut to style my face. So instead of cutting the wig herself, she has a friend of hers trim it to suit my face. She does this because she herself is not familiar with fake hair wigs and doesn't know how to cut them. I am so touched by her professionalism and her concern. She stands there the whole time, observing while her friend cuts the wig while it is on my head, when in reality, she could be earning money working on a different client. She doesn't charge me for either shaving my head (later when my hair starts falling out) or the trim on the wig.

I'm still working hard at my "job" every day doing nothing. I asked my oncologist to refer me to a psychologist. He had suggested that this might be something I may need during this journey. I'm depressed roughly half the time now. My thoughts are consumed by this disease, its implications, and the limitations on my life, what the future holds. I need to crowd my brain with some positive thoughts.

I start seeing this psychologist because I was an executive programs manager with several program managers working for me and now I'm basically doing nothing every day and to top it off I can hardly eat anything. It's strange, but who's responsible for telling the patient not to work any longer? Who even asks what the patient is doing every day?

We have our first appointment and she turns out to be a really down-to-earth person and someone with whom I can really relate.

Radiation treatments have been extended from 5-6 weeks to 7 weeks due to the additional lymph nodes in my neck that the PET scan revealed.

Mental Imagery during the chemo-therapy treatments: My older sister, Chris, suggested I imagine Pac-Men (I know I'm dating myself!) eating away the cancer while I was having the chemo treatment. So now I'm on the Third Stage of "Bargaining" of Elisabeth Kubler Ross's definition of Death and Dying. I'll try anything; just make this go away quickly. Not sure why I hit the Fourth Stage of Depression before the Third; but again, maybe people don't progress in exactly the assigned order.

The other thing I did during the treatments was to listen to my favorite music, especially upbeat, happy music that used to always make me jump up and sing or dance; of course not in the chemo room, but in my head. And you know what? Maybe I should have jumped up and danced! I've recently seen videos of women about to undergo mastectomies, who have the entire surgical staff dancing hysterically to great music prior to their surgeries.

July 30: We had to take Dad to the airport tonight. He has a doctor appointment he can't miss and had to return to California. I don't think I even asked him what appointment that was. Was I that self-absorbed? He told me before he left "I really hate to leave you". He doesn't often show affection, so that was surprising. Mom and Dad haven't been separated from each other very often in the fifty years they have been together. This is such a sacrifice they are enduring to not be in their own comfortable home, but to be here with me.

Today was the second day of radiation and it only took 30 minutes this time. It should only take 15 minutes each time from here on out. Then I drag my tired body and my IV pole back to the chemo room for that wonderful treatment.

July 31: Saturday: Was really tired today and had to force myself to do chores, then had to stop and rest a couple of times. It went so much faster with Mom's help.

August 1: Sunday: Mom and I go to the 8:00 church service today. I do a few easy chores, ironing, watering plants, etc. It seems strange not to have my head stuck in a book studying for the MBA. I've never been one to sit around all day, so this fatigue is really taxing on me. It's hard to just lay or sit down all day and not get things done.

August 3: I contacted an attorney to draw up my will and cremation procedures. She brought the papers over for me to sign. I'm glad that's taken care of. Now I just need to make the arrangements for my cremation and ashes to be placed at Evergreen Conference Center at Oakhurst. You know, that just seemed like something I needed to take care of. Not that I would soon need any of it. I was just being so pragmatic.

Mom must have told my siblings how serious the situation is because my younger sister came to visit. She left, then some time later my brother, his wife and their first child came to visit, then they left and finally my older sister and her husband came to visit. I remember cooking, but couldn't eat much.

August 5: Long day. I had radiation at 8:15, then an appointment with my chemo oncologist at 9:00, chemo at 9:30 for 4 ½ hours. Unusual, because the routine has previously been to start with doctor appointment, then have chemo, then drag me to radiation.

After all that, Mom and I looked at human hair wigs. The lady was a bit rude and only sold long hair wigs. I can't see wasting a long hair wig that someone has taken the time to grow and having me cut it short. I just feel like I'm too old for long hair.

August 6: Had a follow-up appointment with a rheumatologist about the coldness in the fingers of my hands. She seems to be backing off the Reynaud's theory. I think she's been collaborating with my oncologists and has decided we need to get through the cancer treatments before trying to solve this "inconsequential" by-product. She's increased the Cozaar to the max dosage of 100 mg/day. If, after two weeks there has been no change, she wants to call the hand surgeon because she thinks there is a procedure they can do that will open up the blood vessels. Personally, I think the circulation problem is related to the cancer and once the cancer starts dying off, the circulation will improve. Dr. Nix. Just FYI, Dr. Nix is incorrect. Fast forward to 2014 and my index fingers are still so painful and cold all the time. Interestingly enough, the only time they are warm is when I am prone.

The cancer clinic hosted a "Makeup Party" for the patients currently receiving chemo-therapy. They taught us how to apply makeup and to use only new makeup so that we don't get any infections from previously used makeups since our immune systems are compromised. They had scarves and hats for us to try on. Most of the patients had already lost their hair and one person asked me how long I'd been receiving chemo-therapy (to gauge where I was in the hair losing game). I was feeling pretty darned lucky since I was behind the curve and I'd been having chemo for about five weeks. And I remember thinking I didn't have to worry about getting cooties from anyone's head by trying on hats and scarves since most of the patients were sans-hair!

Dad returns tonight. I know my parents really missed each other. For a couple that is not very demonstrative, they sure did show it this past week and it sure is sweet to see.

I still can't believe how well I'm doing. Considering the many, many tests, 3 surgeries, chemo, radiation, not to mention the mental aspect, I'm surprised I'm feeling so well. I really think my overall health, running every day, eating right, prayers, continuing to work and positive attitude are all in my favor. Hooray!

COMIC RELIEF:

A married couple is driving along a highway doing a steady forty miles per hour. The wife is behind the wheel. Her husband, a divorce lawyer, suddenly looks across at her and speaks in a clear voice, "Darling," he says. "I know we've been married for twenty-five years, but I want a divorce." The wife says nothing, keeps looking at the road ahead but slowly increases her speed to 45 mph. "I don't want you to try and talk me out of it", he says, "because I've been having an affair with your best friend, and she's a far better lover than you are." Again the wife stays quiet, but grips the steering wheel more tightly and slowly increases the speed to 55. The husband confidently says, "I want the house." The wife knows he has the skill to get the upper hand in a divorce proceeding. Up to 60. "I want the car, too," he continues. 65 mph. "And," he says, "I want the bank accounts, all the credit cards and the boat." The car veers towards a massive concrete bridge. This makes the husband nervous, so he asks her: "Is there anything you want?" The wife at last replies – in a quiet and controlled voice. "No, I've got everything I need." she says. "Oh, really?" he says with derision. "So what have you got?" Just before they slam into the wall at 65 mph, the wife turns to him and smiles. "The airbag."

CHAPTER 6

And it Gets Tougher

AUGUST 13: CHEMO and radiation treatments yesterday. They added a new drug that prevents damage to the kidney. I had to lay with my head lower than my feet for about 40 minutes while they took my blood pressure every five minutes. When I was finally able to get up, I felt nauseated. That was the one and only time I had to do that procedure.

For the umpteenth time during this journey, I just accepted what I was told to do and didn't ask why that particular drug, why I had to lay in that awkward position. The thing is I felt so vulnerable, scared and ignorant. I viewed the doctors as the authority figures and whatever he or she says must be gospel and I must obey to survive. But I should have asked what this drug was, what the implications were, why I had to have it administered at this particular time, etc., etc., etc.,

That night, I woke up in extreme pain in my chest and back, a very, very sore throat all the way down to my tummy and achy all over, like the flu. The new drug they added yesterday? After radiation the next day, I asked to speak with one of the oncologists who explained that that phenomenon is natural to occur within 24 hours of treatment and didn't say anything about any new treatment. She spent quite some time explaining what to expect–that the pain will get much worse, don't be afraid to take any pain meds, drink the Mary's Magic, etc., and start eating softer, high in fat and protein foods. Mary's Magic is one of the many concoctions invented to numb the throat from the radiation burns so that you can get food down.

She introduced herself and said "you don't know me, but I know you. In fact all the partners of your radiation oncologist are familiar with your case because it is so complicated and your radiation oncologist wanted us all to be familiar with your case". I should have asked what is making my case so complex. She did mention that my radiation covers an unusually large area, including the entire esophagus from my throat to my tummy, which is what is causing the esophagitis (inability to swallow anything).

August 17: When I woke up this morning, I noticed my hair on the pillow. This appears to be the beginning of the end of my hair. How crushing for a female. At the time, I just remember thinking this is part of the procedure and I'll get beyond it. The next morning, I mentioned my hair loss to my mom, but I'm not sure she appreciated the magnitude of the situation and that my all my hair would eventually fall out and I would be totally bald. Maybe she was in denial?

Mom and Dad left today to go to Georgia to visit my sister, Chris. I think they feel rather helpless when they're not here with me and feel better when they can see me and can do things for me. But I'm such a loner and the type of person that rejuvenates by being alone and having quiet time, rather than those who rejuvenate by being surrounded constantly by other people.

It's good timing for them to leave because of my hair falling out. At least my folks don't have to watch that aspect of this horrendous process.

I called Dubbie (Bonett), my hair stylist, and made an appointment to have my head shaved. It's so difficult for her due to the fact that her son had leukemia, underwent chemo and she had had to shave his head. We both cried.

I didn't bother putting makeup on once my hair fell out. I just didn't see the point since the only places I went to were the grocery store, church and the cancer clinic.

You know how you walk into a room and can't remember why you're there? This house is a two story house, with the master bedroom upstairs, and a basement below the ground level (so really three levels). As tired as I am, I make double sure I know where I'm going and why, because it's just too difficult to get somewhere knowing I still have to make it back to another level with or without what I came to get.

I'm eating only soft baby foods now. My doctors have prescribed four different throat medicines to ease the food down. This last one has codeine and is only mildly better than the previous ones. Sitting in the grocery store pharmacy, the pharmacist was so compassionate and asked how I was doing. She said she'd noticed all the drugs that had been prescribed (not to mention the lack of hair) and was hoping that I was improving. Hardly. Little did I know, but there was still so much more to go.

14 radiations down, 19 to go. Counting helps. When I've completed more than half, it'll be a milestone.

Liz suggested I write a book from my journal. I've never been very creative, so I'll have to think about it. Maybe the journal will be enough.

The whole time I was going through my treatments, I thought that if I died, that would be my destiny. To prepare, I completed my will, bought my plot and paid for my cremation. Then I focused on positive attitude, praying to the Lord, and doing everything my doctors said to do. Lots of people prayed for me, the St. Nicholas Church in my home town of Atwater, the many, many people at my company and the people at my local Holy Cross Episcopal Church in Indianapolis. My mom is convinced that is what saved me. Her faith is amazing.

Interestingly enough, I did not tell anyone at the Holy Cross Church where I was attending that I had cancer. I just didn't want any sympathy; I wanted to be known as a normal, healthy person. However, once the swallowing got too bad, I had to ask the Priest to give me very small portions of the bread during the Eucharist and she never asked why. Even when I got the blood infection and had a huge fever blister on my lip she still didn't ask what was wrong. I wonder if she thought it was aids.

August 18: My handwriting is terrible. My index fingers still hurt, but aren't deteriorating any more noticeably. Yeah!

August 20: Yesterday was the big treatment day with both chemo and radiation and I was really afraid I'd wake up in pain again. However, I slept through the night but when I got up, the throat pain started.

I'm now on the 5th different bottle of throat numbing concoction. This one works better than the others, but is absolutely nasty to swallow.

CHRISTIAN RELIEF:

A Baby's Hug

We were the only family with a child in the restaurant. I sat Erik in a high chair and noticed everyone was quietly eating and talking. Suddenly, Erik squealed with glee and said, "Hi there." He pounded his fat baby hands on the high chair tray. His eyes were crinkled in laughter and his mouth was bared in a toothless grin as he wriggled and giggled with merriment.

I looked around and saw the source of his merriment. It was a man whose pants were baggy with a zipper at half-mast and his toes poked out of would-be shoes. His shirt was dirty and his hair was uncombed and unwashed. His whiskers were too short to be called a beard and his nose was so varicose it looked like a road map. We were too far from him to smell, but I was sure he smelled.

His hands waved and flapped on loose wrists. "Hi ya, buster," the man said to David. My husband and I exchanged looks, "What do we do?" David continued to laugh and answer, "Hi, hi there." Everyone in the restaurant noticed and looked at us and then at the man. The old geezer was creating a nuisance with my beautiful baby. Our meal came and the man began shouting from across the room, "Do ya patty cake? Do you know peek-a-boo? Hey, look, he knows peek-a-boo."

Nobody thought the old man was cute. He was obviously drunk. My husband and I were embarrassed. We ate in silence, all except for David, who was running through his repertoire for the admiring skid row bum, who in turn, reciprocated with his cute comments. We finally got through the meal and headed for the door. My husband went to pay the check and told me to meet him in the parking lot.

The old man sat poised between me and the door. "Lord, just let me out of here before he speaks to me or David," I prayed. As I drew closer to the man, I turned my back trying to sidestep him and avoid any air he might be breathing. As I did, David leaned over my arm, reaching with both arms in a baby's "pick-me-up" position. Before I could stop him, David had propelled himself from my arms to the man's. Suddenly a very old smelly man and a very young baby consummated their love relationship. David in an act of total trust, love, and submission laid his tiny head upon the man's ragged shoulder. The man's eyes closed, and I saw tears hover beneath his lashes. His aged hands full of grime, pain, and hard labor, cradled my baby's bottom and stroked his back. No two beings have ever loved so deeply for so short a time. I stood awestruck. The old man rocked and cradled David in his arms and his eyes opened and set squarely on mine. He said in a firm commanding voice, "You take care of this baby." Somehow I managed, "I will," from a throat that contained a stone. He pried David from his chest unwillingly, longingly, as though he were in pain.

I received my baby, and the man said, "God bless you, ma'am, you've given me my Christmas gift." I said nothing more than a muttered thanks. With David in my arms, I ran for the car. My husband was wondering why I was crying and holding David so tightly and why I was saying, "My God, my God, forgive me."

I had just witnessed Christ's love shown through the innocence of a tiny child who saw no sin, who made no judgment; a child who saw a soul, and a mother who saw a suit of clothes. I was a Christian who was blind, holding a child who was not. I felt it was God asking, "Are you willing to share your son for a moment?" when He shared His for all eternity. The ragged old man unwittingly, had reminded me, "To enter the Kingdom of God, we must become as little children."

CHAPTER 7

The Ups and Downs

I WORE MY wig to work today for the first time. I really thought no one noticed until I walked out at the end of the day and the security guard said "I like your hair".

Wednesday the Firefinder team (one of the programs which we are managing was named after the product Firefinder) from work sent me a bouquet of flowers and a card. It was very timely because I was feeling particularly depressed.

I'm still getting "Get Well" cards from the great people at my company every single day. I have a basketful of them. The support, concern and offers of help have been overwhelming. This is a continuation of the system we started at work with the Women's Network caring for and sending cards to those who are sick. Thanks to the Women's Network and other caring fellow employees, I received over 100 cards during my journey.

There has been one friend, Eric, who has stopped by on a number of occasions to talk or bring me things. One time, he brought a dessert which was absolutely heavenly and very rich. I think he knew I was unable to eat and was losing weight and thought the dessert would help. That was so very thoughtful of him (actually I'm sure his wife made the dessert). And to this day, he still remembers my birthday and stays in touch.

I just got off the phone with Mary, my best friend in California. She has been a rock, calling me every Friday to see how I'm doing. It is always good to talk with her.

I didn't know it at the time but she lost her mother to cancer. Then after I had returned to California, she lost her father also to cancer and she didn't tell me until after my treatments and it looked like I would survive.

My son, Ashley, calls at least a couple of times a week. I think he's handling this well, probably because he's not here to see how I'm doing/not doing and is as ignorant as I was about the pain and the implications of the treatments. It's actually not the cancer that hurts, but the treatments and their results to the body.

August 23: The tiredness was overwhelming. I couldn't go to work today. I had radiation and met with my radiation oncologist. Unfortunately, as soon as he walked in the door, I started boo-hooing about the severe pain in my throat and chest. He put me on oxycodone, a pain killer. I can take up to three in three hours. They make me very sleepy.

August 24: I couldn't go to work again and was not able to eat much. I thought I'd start recording my diet each day:

B: Scrambled egg with cheese
L: Jell-O, cheesecake
D: N/A

August 25:
B: N/A
L: Jell-o
D: Boost

I went to work for about three hours. Today, the clinic changed the angles at which they radiate. There are now two on the front and two on the back and the total duration of radiation is twice as long. Again, another example of a change in the routine that I wasn't made aware of ahead of time and probably a good thing because then I would have obsessed about that instead of focusing on my strength and eating properly.

My company has a policy called "catastrophic leave" which they let me take advantage of, and which allows me to be paid while having my treatments. Since I wasn't smart enough to sign up for long term disability, I'm on short term disability which will only last for six months, so every little bit helps.

August 7: Received some bad news yesterday. A friend of mine at work, who has been free of stage I breast cancer for two years has now been told her cancer has progressed to lung, lymph node and liver stage IV cancer. How does that happen? I just do not understand. She said they gave her 12-18 months, with treatments.

August 8: During one of my first chemo treatments, a gentleman came up to me and encouraged me to hang in there. He stated that he had also been diagnosed with lung cancer but was now "cured". So I asked him why he was at the clinic and he replied that they found a small spot on his liver and they were "taking care of it". I only saw him once or twice after that.

August 26:

Thursday is becoming the day of the week that I dread. This time I vomited during chemo. The nurse said they gave me the next drug after the anti-nausea drug too soon and said this is unusual and shouldn't happen again. And guess what, I AGAIN didn't ask why that happened, what drugs, etc. I remember being so embarrassed sitting there vomiting with all the other patients in the room. I felt bad for them that they had to sit there and listen to that. It's not like they can grab their IV pole and run out of the room.

My chemo oncologist omitted the taxol today because my throat and chest hurt so badly. I wondered why because it is the radiation burn and not the chemo that is causing the pain in my throat and chest.

I did some research on the most successful cancer clinics and ran across M.D. Anderson as being renowned for their treatments. Then I talked with my oncologist about getting treatments at M.D. Anderson. In retrospect, I think I might have offended him, making him think I wasn't happy with the treatments he was prescribing when that wasn't the case. He said they wouldn't accept me while I'm undergoing treatment, but that if I wasn't satisfied with the results when the treatments stop, I could consider going there.

We talked about my inability to eat. He wants me to call him on Monday and let him know how I was able to eat over the weekend. He suggested either intravenous feeding thru my port or a feeding tube. Feeding tube sounds grossly gross. I don't think I can do that one.

B Jell-O
L ½ Boost (vomited during chemo)
D 1/3 c. chicken broth

August 27:
B ¼ c. Jell-O, burned throat, chest
L 6 bites each creamed spinach, baby food, 2 oz. applesauce
D ½ c. chicken noodle soup

I've gotten very comfortable about not having hair. The other day one of the guys who used to work for me dropped some work off for me (ha ha ha, like I'm really doing any work anymore) and I forgot I had nothing on my head. Bless his heart; it didn't seem to faze him. In retrospect, I think his visit was just a ploy to stop by and check up on me. In reality, my replacement should be able to sign/handle anything that comes up during the day. But seriously, how sweet that was to come by and check on me!

I am just so tired all the time, I get up in the morning, brush my teeth, then go downstairs, turn on the TV and lay on the couch all day. I'm trying to adjust to the changes to my body and self-image. Being so tired makes it hard for you to get up every morning and try to put on a face when you have no hair and no energy.

My Uncle Tom from England called Tuesday and said he wanted to come visit me. I told him absolutely, and then began worrying about how much I can't do, eat, etc. Mom told me tonight that she called him back and suggested he not come at this time, but maybe when the radiation is over. For that I'm grateful. I just can't entertain right now, even though I'd love to see him again. He's always been my absolute favorite uncle.

I actually felt half human today and worked 7 hours. Felt good.

August 28:
B: nada
L: ¼ c. Swiss soup, slice bread w/peanut butter
D: 6 oz. boost, Jell-O

August 29:
B: 2 pancakes!
L: 2 crackers and cheese
D: 2/3 c. macaroni & cheese

I now realize that I ate too many carbs and not enough veggies and protein, which my body really needed and which my doctors told me many times to concentrate on, but I went for taste and soft, comfort foods that I could get down.

I went to church today, 8:00 service.

August 30:
B: Jell-O
L: peanut butter & jelly sandwich
D: small piece frozen pizza

Can you believe the food I was able to eat??? In hindsight, I should have listened to the doctors and filled up on proteins and fruits and veggies instead of all those carbs, but the comfort food tasted good. And food is so hard to get down, the softer it is, the easier I can get it down.

I went to work today, but don't know why I keep doing this. There is not much for me to do. I guess I'm trying to keep my life as normal as it used to be.

Mary continues to call me every Friday night. It meant a lot to me to stay connected with someone close to me. She sent me a two pound box of See's Candies. I couldn't eat them, but was able to share them with my project managers at work.

I had an appointment with my Rheumatologist today. The cozaar is not working, so I no longer need to take those pills. She suggested we table the idea of any kind of surgery at this point in time. I realize this is because there is no way I can sustain the treatments and undergo some type of surgery.

August 31: I woke up every 3 hours in pain last night and took a pain pill each time.

I went to work at 7:30, and then went to my appointment with the psychologist. I'm going to like her-she really nailed my situation, my independence. She asked "what is the worst thing happening to you right now?" Immediately my response was "the pain". She made me realize my body is trying to fight a tremendous fight right now and I'm not building any energy reserves to allow that to happen. I go to work, not eat, suffer pain or stay home, rest, take pain pills and try to eat. I realize she is completely right and so I go back to work, pack my briefcase and come home. Thankfully, this is my last day at work.

It's now been about 6 weeks since the chemo and radiation began.

B, L, D = ½ Boost (nutrient filled beverage)

September 1: I woke up every 1-2-3 hours last night in pain and tried taking two pain pills to see if I could go back to sleep, but could only sleep for about three hours.

I'm going to have to speak to a doctor about this pain. I just want to make sure they know how very bad it hurts and that I can't get anything but water and Boost down and even that hurts badly. And then the burps and hiccups all day long just reverse the pain, starting in my chest and coming back up.

B, L, D = ½ Boost

COMIC RELIEF:

Airline cabin announcements:

1. On one particular flight passengers were apparently having a hard time choosing their seats, when a flight attendant announced, "People, people, we're not picking out furniture here, find a seat and get in it!"
2. On another flight, with a very "senior" flight attendant crew, the pilot said, "Ladies and gentlemen, we've reached cruising altitude and will be turning down the cabin lights. This is for your comfort and to enhance the appearance of your flight attendants."
3. On landing, the Flight Attendant said, "Please be sure to take all of your belongings. If you're going to leave anything, please make sure it's something we'd like to have."
4. "There may be 50 ways to leave your lover, but there are only 4 ways out of this airplane"

5. "Thank you for flying our airlines. We hope you enjoyed giving us the business as much as we enjoyed taking you for a ride."
6. As the plane landed and was coming to a stop at Ronald Reagan, a lone voice came over the loudspeaker: "Whoa, big fella. WHOA!"
7. After a particularly rough landing during thunderstorms in Memphis, a flight attendant on a Northwest flight announced, "Please take care when opening the overhead compartments because, after a landing like that, sure as heck everything has shifted."
8. From an airlines employee: "Welcome aboard Flight 876 to Tampa: To operate your seat belt, insert the metal tab into the buckle, and pull tight. It works just like every other seat belt; and, if you don't know how to operate one, you probably shouldn't be out in public unsupervised."
9. "In the event of a sudden loss of cabin pressure, masks will descend from the ceiling. Stop screaming, grab the mask, and pull it over your face. If you have a small child traveling with you, secure your mask before assisting with theirs. If you are traveling with more than one small child, pick your favorite."
10. "Weather at our destination is 50 degrees with some broken clouds, but we'll try to have them fixed before we arrive. Thank you, and remember, nobody loves you, or your money, more than our airline."
11. "Your seat cushions can be used for flotation; and, in the event of an emergency water landing, please paddle to shore and take them with our compliments."
12. "As you exit the plane, make sure to gather all of your belongings. Anything left behind will be distributed evenly among the flight attendants. Please do not leave children or spouses."
13. And from the pilot during his welcome message: "our airline is pleased to have some of the best flight attendants in the industry. Unfortunately, none of them are on this flight!"
14. Heard on a plane just after a very hard landing: The flight attendant came on the intercom and said, "That was quite a bump, and I know what y'all are thinking. I'm here to tell you it wasn't the airline's fault, it wasn't the pilot's fault, it wasn't the flight attendant's fault, it was the asphalt."
15. Overheard on a flight into Amarillo, Texas, on a particularly windy and bumpy day: During the final approach, the Captain was really having to fight it. After an extremely hard landing, the Flight Attendant said, "Ladies and Gentlemen, welcome to Amarillo. Please remain in your seats with your seat belts fastened while the Captain taxis what's left of our airplane to the gate!"
16. Another flight attendant's comment on a less than perfect landing: "We ask you to please remain seated as Captain Kangaroo bounces us to the terminal."

17. An airline pilot wrote that on this particular flight he had hammered his ship into the runway really hard. The airline had a policy which required the first officer to stand at the door while the passengers exited, smile, and give them a "Thanks for flying our airline." He said that, in light of his bad landing, he had a hard time looking the passengers in the eye, thinking that someone would have a smart comment. Finally everyone had gotten off except for a little old lady walking with a cane. She said, "Sir, do you mind if I ask you a question?" "Why, no, Ma'am," said the pilot. "What is it?" The little old lady said, "Did we land, or were we shot down?"

18. After a real crusher of a landing in Phoenix, the attendant came on with, "Ladies and Gentlemen, please remain in your seats until Capt. Crash and the Crew have brought the aircraft to a screeching halt against the gate. And, once the tire smoke has cleared and the warning bells are silenced, we'll open the door and you can pick your way through the wreckage to the terminal."

19. Part of a flight attendant's arrival announcement: "We'd like to thank you folks for flying with us today. And, the next time you get the insane urge to go blasting through the skies in a pressurized metal tube, we hope you'll think of our airline"

20. Heard on a flight. "Ladies and gentlemen, if you wish to smoke, the smoking section on this airplane is on the wing and if you can light 'em, you can smoke 'em."

CHAPTER 8

Sometimes it Gets Worse

I WENT FOR radiation today but when I got on the table, I must have panicked. My chest hurt so badly and I kept swallowing, making it worse. They took me off the table and I didn't get radiation today. Afterward, I spoke with one of the oncologists who had me get an esophogram at Community North. The esophogram came out normal, thank goodness. Tomorrow, we'll talk about where to go from here, a feeding tube, etc. I tried eating some chicken broth, but could only get a few sips down.

My oncologist describes that I have Protein Calorie Malnutrition (PCM) as a result of my inability to intake food and liquids. He recommends inserting nutrients into my port so that I can get the basic nutrients I need to function.

September 7: A nurse comes by the house to show me how to utilize the nutrient bag and how to hook it up to my port. In retrospect I realize I didn't retain much of what she said. Probably most importantly I didn't pay attention to how to clean my port each time and keep the end cap on. Not doing so is probably what caused me to acquire a blood infection called Klebsiella. Each night, I take a bag out of the refrigerator, attach it to my port and turn on the pump. During the night, the liquid is pumped into my body to replenish the needed nutrients.

Each morning I get up feeling so nauseous and full. It's disgusting for someone who SO appreciates the taste of well cooked food to receive liquid food into the body that has no flavor or taste or appreciation.

My mom's journal indicates I threw up quite a bit during the next several days, but I don't remember any of that. Interesting what we block out.

September 13: Wow, it's been a while. After my last radiation attempt, the oncologist prescribed hospitalization to let me get some relief from the pain, to get some nutrients into my body and to replenish the dehydration. I spent the next 6 days in the hospital. My goal of course was to get the pain under control. The hospital won. I gained 4 lbs., but they did not get the pain under control. I don't remember anything about this hospital stay. I was on morphine the whole time and then they prescribed morphine patches after I left. Later, I was to remember two co-workers of mine coming to visit me in the hospital, but I remember nothing about the visit. They must have felt so uncomfortable not being able to talk to me or do anything for me.

I haven't had chemo since August 26, which has been a welcome relief. My chemo oncologist felt it was doing more harm than good right now. Actually, it was the radiation burning my insides, not allowing me to eat or drink anything. Now I worry that I'm losing valuable chemo time.

There is a big sale at Lazarus tomorrow. I know I shouldn't be spending so much money, but these are things I want, things I'll enjoy using when I can eat again. I started my collection of china, silver and stemware. Feminine Modano Lace china. Gotta love it.

Short term disability will only pay 50% of my income, so I should be rationing my money accordingly, but darned if I'm doing that. However, I am re-financing the house which will help.

My thinking has been that this cancer is a short term problem. I'll do my radiation and chemo, and then be done. But then?? What if I don't make it??

I haven't entertained that thought at all so far. I'd like to be prepared for either eventuality, not quite sure how to do that, though.

Self Help Groups: There are plenty out there. I was just too tired, too much in pain and too self-absorbed to drag myself out in public to discuss how tired and in pain I was and actually couldn't see any benefit to my condition. Again, different treatments cause different reactions. My treatment was pretty aggressive with chemo every week for six months, simultaneously with 33 days of radiation. So just be aware that your situation may be quite different and likely easier.

September 20: In my mind, I'm thinking let's get this treatment over with so I can get back to work! My mom and I take some of my suits to a tailor to have them taken in since I've lost so much weight. On the way home, I hit a curb and my attitude was so "what-ever". I wasn't worried about the car or curb, but more so about losing control over my faculties. Then as we got into my sub-division I remember thinking, I'm going to hit that mailbox. And boom, I hit it. It did no damage to the mailbox, but I had to replace my rearview mirror. Later, I mentioned it to my oncologist and he remarked that the chemo can have adverse effects on the eyesight.

COMIC RELIEF:

An older lady gets pulled over for speeding . . .

Older Woman: Is there a problem, Officer? Officer: Ma'am, you were speeding. Older Woman: Oh, I see. Officer: Can I see your license please? Older Woman: I'd give it to you but I don't have one. Officer: Don't have one? Older Woman: Lost it, 8 years ago for drunk driving. Officer: I see . . . Can I see your vehicle registration papers please. Older Woman: I can't do that. Officer: Why not? Older Woman: I stole this car. Officer: Stole it? Older Woman: Yes, and I killed and hacked up the owner. Officer: You what? Older Woman: His body parts are in plastic bags in the trunk if you want to see. The Officer looks at the woman and slowly backs away to his car and calls for back up. Within minutes 4 police cars circle the car. A senior officer slowly approaches the car, clasping his half drawn gun. Officer 2: Ma'am, could you step out of your vehicle please! The woman steps out of her vehicle.

Older woman: Is there a problem sir? Officer 2: One of my officers told me that you have stolen this car and murdered the owner. Older Woman: Murdered the owner? Officer 2: Yes, could you please open the trunk of your car, please. The woman opens the trunk, revealing nothing but an empty trunk. Officer 2: Is this your car, ma'am? Older Woman: Yes, here are the registration papers. The officer is quite stunned. Officer 2: One of my officers claims that you do not have a driving license. The woman digs into her handbag and pulls out a clutch purse and hands it to the officer. The officer examines the license. He looks quite puzzled. Officer 2: Thank you ma'am, one of my officers told me you didn't have a license, that you stole this car, and that you murdered and hacked up the wner. Older Woman: Bet the liar told you I was speeding, too.

CHAPTER 9

And Worse

SEPTEMBER 25: IT'S been an eventful past ten days or so. I'll try to start from ten days ago and recreate.

This past Monday was a milestone because I finally finished radiation. The last three sessions I received six zaps instead of the usual four. The doctors said to expect two days of recovery for every one day of radiation, so that's a total of 66 days of recovery. They made a big show of giving me a certificate stating I'd completed the 33 days of radiation. Honestly, the more appropriate reward would have been a new throat or maybe a million dollars or a Jaguar.

Monday evening I went to bed and had the chills and shakes. I didn't think too much about it because it has happened once before about 3-4 weeks ago and only lasted that one night. Then, Tuesday night, same thing. I finally got to sleep after several hours only to awake again with chills and shakes. This time I got up, put on more clothes and blankets and took some Morgan's solution. Morgan's solution is a concoction of numbing agents intended to numb the pain in my throat so I can get food down. It only lasts for 4-5 swallows, so it's virtually ineffective. I don't know why I took that because it wasn't going to do anything for the chills and shakes.

Wednesday was my appointment with the psychologist. During that appointment, I got the chills again. I have to say, this doctor has been very perceptive and has given me sound advice that I have followed. She immediately called the cancer clinic and described my condition. They said to bring me in right away. Then she called Dad and asked him to pick me up and take me to the clinic.

At the clinic I walked in with Dad, but when I got to the counter, the nurse, said, "Susan, you are spilling your water". I had a thermal cup of water and wasn't aware I wasn't holding the cup properly. Then I collapsed and someone brought a wheelchair and placed me in it. I was taken to a private bed and my temperature was taken numerous times. I was chastised for not having taken my temperature. Who knew? I never felt like I had a fever because I was so cold.

My fever got as high as 105.7 and my blood pressure as low as 50 something over 30 something. I was told I went into septic shock. (When I get home I'm going to look that up). Many people die from septic shock. I've been told several times that I'm lucky to be alive. I had no idea.

You're given so much reading material when you first begin treatments and I read it all. But with the chemo brain and my natural tendency to forget, I didn't recall the part about chills and shakes, but sure enough, it was there.

Mom and I have decided that regardless of how I feel from now on; I'll be taking my temperature every day.

From the clinic I was taken by ambulance to the hospital and placed in the intensive care unit (ICU). I hate hospitals. They're like prisons. I have little memory of the three days I spent in ICU except taking off my clothes, putting on the gown, and then being able to walk around when I felt better. They gave me blood transfusions, which stabilized me, but it took three days. My radiation oncologist came to see me, even though I was no longer having the radiation. That was very considerate of him.

After ICU, I am put into a room with a 66 year old woman who is almost totally deaf. Everyone has to shout to communicate with her. And they can't check my vitals when they check hers in the middle of the night. Oh no. They wake her with yelling which coincidentally wakes me. Then two hours later, just after I've finally fallen back asleep, it's mysteriously time to check my vitals!

Today she took a shower (boy, was I jealous since I could only take bird baths because of the needle in my chest) and put some kind of perfume on that stunk up the room something fierce. That was three hours ago and the room still stinks. Then she turned the thermostat down to about 50 degrees. My folks and I were all bundled up with coats and blankets. We complained to the nurse and she adjusted the thermostat. And when my roommate has visitors, she has visitors and I mean many!

Her doctor came in to discuss her diagnoses with her, which turned out to be gall stones.

I immediately recognized him as the physician who installed my port. What a coinkidink! She says something like "you a baby, how old is you?" (You go girl, same thing I thought when I first met him! Turns out he's an awesome surgeon.) He tells her she needs surgery to remove the gall stones and her response was "I's

60 years old, I ain't havin' no surgery, I's too old." As of the writing of this book in 2014, I am about to turn 59 years old. I hope I don't ever get too old to believe I can't survive a necessary surgery. My roommate is still a sweetheart in my mind, just not very confident.

Today is Saturday and I'm told I'm here for the weekend. I am going absolutely nuts being confined like this. They've resolved the chills and shakes and I'm feeling much better but they won't let me go until they've identified the type of blood infection. I definitely want to know what the source of this infection is so I don't ever get it again.

Did I mention I hate hospitals? I haven't been as mentally and physically challenged in the past three days since I got out of ICU than I can remember ever before. I try going for a walk outside but the hospital staff doesn't much care for their patients wandering around aimlessly in nothing but a gown and dragging an IV pole. Go figure. So I tried taking walks around the floor, but the adjacent side of the floor is for pediatrics, so I can't walk there.

My legs and ankles are so swollen from all the fluids they're giving me; I can't even cross my legs which is amazing because I'm 5'0", weighing about 95 lbs. and skinny as a rail.

On the positive side, the cafeteria personnel would come to my room each day trying to find something to prepare for me that I could get down my throat. That was so thoughtful.

The nurse comes in and tells me I have to take this pill. I look at it and immediately know that just isn't going to happen; it's just too big. I told her so and she breaks it in half and I'm thinking still no way. She hands me the pill and water and in it goes, but it gets stuck in my throat. I TOLD YOU SO. My dad starts pounding my back because I can't breathe and the pill won't go up or down. The nurse gets angry at him and he tells them to do something, so they stand there and watch me. Eventually all my heaving and coughing ejects the pill and the nice nurse leaves with her hateful (and harmful) pills. And yet another situation where I was told to do something and did it without asking why, what is the pill for, what are the consequences!

Today an absolutely huge basket of plants and a vase of flowers arrived from several coworkers. There were two cards completely covered with signatures. I was so touched and it was very uplifting after the rotten day I've had. I do have to mention that these folks are the wonderful people who work at the Raytheon Indianapolis facility.

I get a call from my boss while I'm in the hospital. He asks if the CEO of our company had sent me an email. Now, there are 80,000 employees in our company; why would I get an email from our CEO??? I haven't even given my email a thought since I left work a couple of weeks ago. Sure enough, I check my blackberry and there is a very compassionate email from our CEO. I'm told he writes his own emails, but who's kidding who? Then I struggle with whether I'm supposed to reply, which I end up doing by saying "That's why I love working for this company because of the compassionate leadership." Then he (or she, whoever) replied again. And I decided that's enough email tag with a busy CEO. Someone obviously notified him of my illness and he felt compelled to send the email (or directed someone to) probably since I'd just met him this year and received the top two awards the company hands out (the CEO and Program Leadership awards).

The absolute maximum number of life days of a needle for my port is seven days. I finally got a new one today. It's been almost two weeks. Uh, isn't that odd. I'd been in the hospital for an infection that was probably caused by my port and they don't bother to replace the needle to my port or ask how long it had been in before being admitted? Since I've been diagnosed with PCM, they leave the tube and needle attached to my port, so I can attach the tubing to the nutrient bag when I go to bed.

The port is a very vulnerable site for infection, no excuses. On one visit to my oncologist, he asked where the plug was for the tube hanging from my port and I didn't even realize it was missing. I need to be more careful. For some reason, I've not been able to view this whole thing as life threatening (still denying?). I've been so sure of a recovery. I've even been buying suits for when I return to work, which is really dumb because I've lost about 20 pounds and am sure to put that back on eventually.

COMIC RELIEF:

Nine people were hanging on a rope under a helicopter – eight men and one woman. The rope was not strong enough to carry them all, so they decided that one had to leave, because otherwise they were all going to fall. They weren't able to name that person, until the woman gave a very touching speech. She said that she would voluntarily let go of the rope, because, as a woman, she was used to giving up everything for her husband and kids, or for men in general, and was used to always making sacrifices with little in return. As soon as she finished her speech, all the men started clapping their hands . . . .

CHAPTER 10

Roller Coaster

I'M CONVINCED, AND so is my chemo oncologist, that the poor circulation in my index finger is a by-product of the tumor. Hopefully, we're both right because I've stopped taking the cozaar that my rheumatologist prescribed.

September 26: Today is my sister Liz's birthday. I have to remember to call her this morning.

Last night my hospital roomie added a new skill to her repertoire for my entertainment pleasure. She exhales through her mouth but her lips flop so it sounds like constant farts.

Actually, I'm still finding her manner of speaking amusing. It's a high pitched, twangy, very deep south, highly un-educated dialect. I wish I could replicate it in writing. It's something like "I's gots to take a bath, I gots no clean clothes. I's goin home". I suppose by the time one of us leaves, I'll be annoyed by it.

Again, when she has visitors, they come in by the dozen, at least. They spill over into my half of the room. And they are so loud. Why can't they speak quietly?

Interestingly enough, I spend my hospital days and even those after I get home, watching the cooking channel, writing down the recipes I'd like to make. Then when I got home, I printed out the dozens and dozens of recipes, waiting until the day when I can cook and really enjoy food again. There was absolutely no doubt in my mind I would get to that place eventually. Focus on your passions!

September 27: There was a big ruckus about the noise my roommate has been causing. I think the folks on the other side of our room/wall complained. They moved her to a private room. Isn't that rich? She's causing the problem and she gets a private room. I finally get one night and a partial day of peace.

I was released from the hospital today. I worried about it all night that my chemo oncologist might want to be his cautious self and keep me longer. As soon as a doctor came by and told me what the blood infection was and that I would be released, I immediately got up, got dressed and called mom and dad to come get me. The nurse came by and indignantly asked me why I was dressed and I explained that the doctor had told me I would be released. She got angry and left the room. It was at least an hour before she would come back to take out the needle in my port and give me the paperwork to go home. Snot.

They found the source of the infection. It is called "klebsiella pneumonia". The doctor could not tell me what caused it other than the fact that my immune system is very vulnerable and I need to be more careful about taking my temperature.

I was just so darned relieved to be going home. First thing I did when I got home was to take a shower. Six days without a shower is a long time. The shower felt so good. So this is the first time without a tube in my chest in about a month. And no more nutrient bag every night!! I can eat whatever I want or can.

For dinner that night, Dad asked what I wanted to eat and I asked for Taco Bell, chicken burrito. I could only eat half of it, but what great comfort food that was! Should have asked for steak and lobster with a twice baked potato and salad!

My handwriting is atrocious and even when I slow down and concentrate it doesn't get any better. It has to be the Reynaud's and unfortunately, this will become a permanent result of this cancer journey.

I have a huge fever blister on top of my nose from the fever last week. Lovely. I've lost almost all of my eyelashes. And so begins the challenge of applying makeup and look like you do have lashes and you're a female.

September 28: What a great day to be alive! The weatherman predicted sunny and 76 degrees. Yet fall is coming.

I need to find spaces in the house for all the outside plants. Not used to this; I used to live in California where the plants stayed outside year round. I received two huge baskets and one large plant since I've been sick and had to find room for them.

I bought a TV for Mom and Dad's bedroom. Thursday, DirecTV is coming to hook up theirs and 2 other TVs to the satellite.

My ankles are huge. I'm sitting here with my legs propped up and everything from my waist down is still swollen from all the liquids in the hospital.

I've learned how little physical imperfections mean anymore. I have no hair on my head, no eyelashes and a huge fever blister on my nose. But I'm alive and feel it. Last week's scare sure brings home what life really means. All the physical stuff will heal. I used to be pretty vain about my appearance so this is a come-uppance for me. Clearly, I'm in the "acceptance" stage.

Tomorrow I see the psychologist again. I brought her an orchid plant to thank her for what she did last week, basically saving my life. I realize it seems kind of a trivial gift in exchange for the gift of life. Maybe I should have given her a million dollars or a Jaguar!

October 2: Not feeling quite right today. Very tired and a little tummy ache. I was cold all day, finally took a shower and put some long johns and sweats on. No fever, thank goodness.

This sure is a roller coaster effect. One day I feel good, the next it's a one eighty. Reminds me of when my son was in boot camp for the Corps and he explained how they take every privilege away from you, and then slowly give it back piece by piece as you earn it. The idea is to teach you the mantra of the Corps: Corps, God, and Country. The Corps takes care of each other above all else. With the cancer/treatments, you get torn down, then get built back up, then down, then up.

Mom and I cleaned the house in preparation for my brother's visit. Then she said Wednesday we'll give the house "a lick and a promise", which is a typical British comment, which means we'll do a light touch up just before he comes.

Tomorrow is church and the weather is supposed to be cold. It's time to pull out the coat and gloves. The cold makes my index fingers hurt something worse than fierce.

Throughout this entire ordeal, I never really wasted much time blaming Christ or bargaining. My approach was very pragmatic and surreal. I've been diagnosed with cancer, the doctors can make it go away and I'll get on with life. But if I don't, I'll get my affairs in order, select my spot at ECCO and pay for my cremation. I purchased my spot as close to my parents' as possible. Check! Those tasks are done. And, no one in the family has to worry about that if the time should come.

It's time to start Christmas shopping. I really need to finish my Uncle Tom and Heidi's package in order to get it to England by Christmas. Every year, the British postal service employees conduct a strike in order to affect higher pay increases since Christmas time is the busiest time of the year. That way, the employees have a good chance of securing the higher wages since the postal service needs them to get through the season.

Tom called today and wants to visit at Christmas. We'll all be at Mom's and the weather will be nicer than in Indiana. It'll be fun.

October 11: Had a lovely visit with Michael, Aimee and Emma. It is also Mom and Dad's wedding anniversary and I didn't even remember and of course they would never say anything. How selfish of me.

Mom and Dad are leaving for home on Wednesday. I only hope I can keep myself healthy enough to stay out of the hospital.

October 15: Not sure why, but now that I'm only on the chemo, I'm so very tired. All I feel like doing is lying down. Interestingly enough, once I get up and start doing something I start to have a little energy.

I've only been getting the taxol and not the cisplatin because my red and white blood cell counts are too low. The chemo kills all the cells, the good ones as well as the bad ones, so eventually the good cells become too depleted and replenishment is required before more killing can occur. So every two weeks I will get a red blood cell shot and every day for the next 6 days a white blood cell shot. Both cause nauseousness and vomiting and I feel a little queasy all day.

COMIC RELIEF:

One Sunday morning, the pastor noticed little Timmy was staring up at the large plaque that hung in the foyer of the church. It was covered with names, and small American flags were mounted oneither side of it. The seven-year-old had been staring at the plaque for some time, so the pastor walked up, stood beside the boy and said quietly, "Good morning Timmy." "Good morning Father," replied the young man, still focused on the plaque "Father McGhee, what is this?" Timmy asked. "Well, son, it's a memorial to all the men and women who have died in the service. Soberly, they stood together, staring at the large plaque. Little Timmy's voice was barely audible when he asked, "Which one, the 9:00 or the 11:00 service?"

CHAPTER 11

On the Mend?

MOM AND DAD left on Wednesday and I have mixed emotions about that. They kept me company and did so much for me for which I'm sure I didn't fully express my appreciation. But I had no time to myself. Hopefully, I will stay healthy until the treatments are over and will be able to go to California for Christmas. Uncle Tom, my son Ash, Lizzie my granddaughter, and Amy my daughter-in-law, will be coming. It'll be so good to see everyone again. Family is everything.

The weather has been so cold, grey and rainy for three days now. I could use some sunshine.

Well, ask and ye shall receive. I just looked up and the sun has come out. Boy is it pretty. Thank you, Jesus.

One of the treats I'm giving the dogs is making Zack pass gas a lot. I have it narrowed down between two culprits, so I'll figure it out.

I received a little depressing news. I talked with my chemo oncologist about determining my progress. I've been doing research and reading books and there is something called blood markers that can indicate how well the treatments are reducing the cancer. However, he said blood markers aren't accurate with lung cancer. He said surgery to remove the tumor isn't viable because "the dispersion of spread is too great". In other words, there are cancerous lymph nodes too far from the source (of the tumor) and you can't perform enough surgery to remove them all. He said our best bet is the radiation and chemo combo. The radiation to reduce/eradicate the cancer, then have the chemo finish off any remaining cancer cells is our best bet.

So just to mess up Elisabeth Kubler Ross's stages of Death and Dying, I guess I'm in a "why me' or Anger stage right now which is the second stage. The prognosis isn't good and everything I suggest to the doctor gets turned down. It doesn't help that almost every day I feel pain for one reason or another.

October 16: Wow, feeling pretty good today. Got up around 7:00 am and just kept going all day. Had my 2nd leukine (white blood cell) shot and had to go to the east side clinic today and tomorrow for the shot since the cancer clinic where I receive treatments, right around the corner from my house, is closed on Saturday and Sunday. And these shots are given in the arm, not the port. So, so painful.

It's cold today–in the 40's. I'm sitting here with a beautiful fire going, a glass of chardonnay and watching the food channel. I'm working up an appetite for dinner by watching the food channel.

It feels so good to eat again. Some things don't taste the same, but most food tastes darned good. I'm not gaining any weight, weighing around 95 lbs., but my clothes feel good and I don't feel skinny. For the first time in my life, I eat anything I want and don't gain weight.

October 22: Well, all my counts were good yesterday, so today they gave me the full meal deal, the full chemo drugs. However, they changed the cisplatin to carboplatin and it only took about 3-4 hours instead of the 6 hours it usually takes. I also didn't get the taxol for some reason (and again I DIDN'T ASK WHY NOT!). My chemo oncologist was out this week and again next week, so I couldn't ask him about the change in drugs, but I could have asked the nurse.

I've always been a very energetic, active person. Work out in the morning, work 9-10 hours/day, come home and do things around the house, then eventually sit down and watch a little TV before going to bed. So, it is so hard sitting at home day after day. I'm so bored. And when I do have something to do, it's difficult to do anything because of the fatigue. Most days I get up, brush my teeth, then go downstairs and lay down on the couch all day, usually watching TV or reading a book, just no energy whatsoever. I just take one day at a time and do what I can. Just another 1 ½-2 months of chemo and we'll know how well the treatments have worked.

They are scheduling a CT scan, mostly for my own gratification, to see how much affect the treatments have had on the cancer. My radiation oncologist warned me, though, that after only a month since finishing the radiation, it could be deceiving. Cancer cells double every 2-3 months and you really need several scans over several months to differentiate scar tissue from potential cancer.

I've decided to renovate the bottom floor of my house, to include the foyer, kitchen, living room, family room and dining room. I'm having bamboo flooring installed throughout, with new granite counter tops installed in the kitchen. The bamboo flooring was delivered this past Monday, but Lowes screwed up on the installation schedule and it won't happen until November 1st through 3rd. Oh well, a couple of weeks after that, the counter tops will be installed so it'll all be done before Thanksgiving. It's going to look so much better and more up-to-date. Right now I have old laminate counter tops and linoleum and carpet flooring.

Spending all this money has not even fazed me. I'm not rich, but am comfortable. The bonuses I've received have been invested. I don't travel or spend money frivolously. Yet, I spent $600 on suits for work, anticipating I'd get back to work after treatments. And will spend $20,000 remodeling the kitchen. The speakers were installed for satellite TV. And I'm on partial disability. The Lord will tell me what to do and when to stop spending. It's almost as if the spending is an investment in my future, sell this home, move somewhere else and serve the Lord.

Tomorrow I'm meeting a former project manager for lunch. He used to work for me and has since retired and moved to Ohio. He then was diagnosed with a tumor behind one of his eyes. Fortunately, he is able to take drugs to reduce the tumor and voila! It's gone. I'm so glad it didn't turn out like Bill and Cindy's diagnosis.

So, a friend of mine at work was diagnosed with breast cancer, another friend with a tumor behind his eye, and another friend of mine with stomach cancer. And me with lung cancer. Come on!! What are the odds?

The weather is beautiful today. I have a couple of windows open and am getting some fresh air in here. I wish I felt like going for a walk.

My radiation oncologist gave me a long speech about eating the right foods to build up my immune system, so I'm trying (who told him about the wine?). I also need to drink lots of water. Fortunately, I've always liked water, so that's not a problem. I'm also trying to keep a dessert around since I can't seem to gain weight (I know, oxymoron). The suits I bought at Lazarus were size 2 and I have to safety pin the waist line to keep them up.

October 29: Cell counts were good yesterday (except hemoglobin) so I got both the taxol and carboplatin. For the hemoglobin, I had to get a shot-the one that hurts.

Last night I had the CT scan so hopefully next week I'll get to see the films. I want to compare them to the ones before treatment started, so I can see for myself what progress has been made.

I went for a walk today with the dogs. I got tired after about ½ block but kept going. I want to build up my leg muscles again. I'm going to try to walk every day.

I also got out and washed the BMW. The weather is really nice and in the low 70s, although we were supposed to get rain today.

My hair seems to be falling out of my head again since I had it shaved a couple of months ago. It's grown out to about ½", but I'm noticing many hairs on my pillowcases. I wish it would either grow or completely fall out. It looks silly as it is. I have eyebrows, but no eyelashes. Go figure.

Yesterday, I received a beautiful bouquet of flowers from Michael & Aimee. That was so thoughtful of them. They must have signed up for some type of program because they said I would receive something each month for 6 months. What a lovely gift.

I don't think a day has gone by that I haven't received a card in the mail from someone. It never ceases to amaze me that people are still thinking about me.

November 8: Treatment last Thursday consisted only of taxol, excluding the carboplatin. White blood cell count was too low, so I get the shots again.

Scottey is having a tooth pulled tomorrow. He broke it somehow and the Vet said it would cause him pain to chew with a broken tooth. So he gets to eat canned food for a week and I had to feed Scottey and Zack separately since they normally eat dry dog food together.

Also tomorrow, I'm having lunch with my friend who has stomach cancer. It'll be good to see him again. We're meeting at Denny's. There isn't much he can keep down, but there are BLTs at Denny's and Steak n Shake that don't make him nauseous.

After lunch, I'm scheduled for a massage. I'm not sure if I should go or not; my chest and back muscles have ached for several days now; not sure how it will feel. A full body massage is something I started treating myself to long before I was diagnosed with cancer and I thoroughly enjoy them.

The weather has been absolutely beautiful for the past couple of weeks. It's supposed to start getting more like November weather by the end of the week.

My reservations are made for December 22-28 to Atwater. It's going to be fun.

My weight is slowly increasing. I was at a low of 94 lbs. and am currently at 99. I'm trying to eat healthy each meal-fruits and veggies, but am also trying to keep a dessert around.

I'm telling myself this entire obsession about weight is influenced by the clinic. Every week, I am weighed and chastised if I lose weight, which is ironic because they are the people that are inflicting the treatments, which have caused the weight loss in the first place! Just looking for someone else to blame besides myself.

My index and third fingers are still cold all the time. After all this radiation and chemo and no appreciable improvement in these two fingers, I guess I'm going to have to have something done about it. When they get extremely cold, they become very painful as well and nothing can relieve the pain except to get the warmth back.

I speak with my sister, my parents, my son, daughter-in-law and granddaughter and we agree to get together for a day since we haven't all been together in months. We decide to meet in Bakersfield for lunch, which is about half way between their town and mine. While waiting for our food to arrive, my sister Liz looked quizically at my normally very straight hair and asked if it had grown back out curly (which it had). I replied yes and she said "well, I guess it was all worth it then?" We all busted up laughing because the journey was so, so difficult and curly hair didn't come close to "making it all worth it". Unfortunately, the curliness didn't stay and I reverted back to my normal straight brown hair. However, I have heard of women whose hair color changed drastically from one color to another when it finally did grow back out. So maybe you'll become a blond!

November 9: Lovely lunch with my friend and his wife. We trade experiences on our cancer journeys and try to stay positive.

The massage was good, but didn't really relieve any of the pain. I guess it's not so much muscle as it is loss of blood cells. My massage therapist is so kind and so Christian and I am grateful to her for the many, many massages I benefited from, previous to the cancer.

November 12: I went to a seminar today entitled "Frankly Speaking about Lung Cancer". It wasn't that great, merely confirmed most of what I already knew. The speaker's studies show <5% survival for stage IIIB after 5 years. Dr. Hardacre gave me 15% survival. Either way I wonder if I should plan on a 5 year survival? The seminar did reinforce that I need to get some kind of consistent exercise such as walking, yoga or Tai Chi. I have a yoga tape (again, this was ten years ago, so I was still using tapes!) I've never used so I think I'll give it a try tomorrow.

Treatment yesterday was just taxol again-no cisplatin or carboplatin. I'm now concerned about not getting the platins.

November 20: I went to church today, and then went to the East clinic for the white blood cell count shot. For some reason, my chemo oncologist changed the shot from Leukine to a different one. No one told me the shot would be different and I DIDN'T ASK WHY! The Leukine didn't hurt at all, but this other one does hurt. I think that's what put me in such a bad mood today. From there I started thinking about my prognosis, especially the one from the seminar last week. If I only have five years or less, how do I want to spend that time? Tomorrow I'm going to check my pension and see what I could get if I retired at 50 or 53.

Well, the flooring installation was supposed to take three days and is now into three weeks and still not done. The quarter round has been ready to install for a week now and I'm still waiting.

The countertops were removed last night and the new ones will be installed tomorrow; then the plumber has to come back to install the new sink and faucet.

November 21: So, I can't get my pension until I turn 55. That's not going to do me much good since that's the end of my five year survival date. Worst case, my beneficiaries will inherit my pension.

COMIC RELIEF:

After getting Pope Jacob's luggage loaded into the limo (and he doesn't travel light), the driver notices that the Pope is still standing on the curb. "Excuse me, Your Eminence," says the driver, "would you please take your seat so we can leave?" "Well, to tell you the truth," says the Pope. "They never let me drive at the Vatican, and I'd really like to drive today." "I'm sorry, but I cannot let you do that. I'd lose my job. And what if something should happen?" protests the driver wishing he'd never gone to work that morning. "There might be something extra in it for you," says the Pope. Reluctantly, the driver gets in the back as the Pope climbs in behind the wheel. The driver quickly regrets his decision when, after exiting the airport, the Supreme Pontiff floors it, accelerating the limo to 105 mph. "Please slow down Your Holiness!!!" pleads the worried driver. But the Pope keeps the pedal to the metal until they hear sirens. "Oh, my God, I'm gonna lose my license," moans the driver. The Pope pulls over and rolls down the window as the cop approaches. But the cop takes one look at him, goes back to his motorcycle, and gets on the radio. "I need to talk to the Chief," he says to the dispatcher. The Chief gets on the radio and the cop tells him that he's stopped a limo going a 105 mph. "So bust him," said the Chief. "I don't think we want to do that. He's really important," said the cop. Chief exclaimed, "All the more reason!!!" "No, I mean REALLY important," said the cop. The Chief then asked, "Who do you have there, the Mayor?" Cop: "Bigger!" Chief: "Premier?" Cop: "Bigger!" "Well," said the Chief, "Who is it?" Cop: "I think it's God!" Chief: "What makes you think it's God?" Cop: "He's got the Pope for a limo driver."

CHAPTER 12

Getting Through the Holidays and Then the Good News

THANKSGIVING WAS GOING to be pretty depressing this year, until Karen invited me to Thanksgiving dinner at her house. She is the Controller (or Chief Financial Officer) at our facility. She has been very compassionate about my condition and she is the one who initiated our Women's Network at our facility. She also invited Sam, a mutual friend and financial analyst and another friend, Irene, whom we all met when the Calgary, Canada facility was built and established. It was very pleasant and a memory I'll chuckle about for a long time. Dinner was to be at 3:00, but the turkey wasn't done till 6:00. So we had salad, then bread, then dessert, then finally the turkey. Everything was delish and Irene kept us entertained all day with her stories of farm life.

December 7: Pearl Harbor Day. I heard on Fox News this morning that more people were killed on 9/11 than on Pearl Harbor Day. I didn't realize that.

I'm so tired of being tired. The interesting thing is that once I convince myself to get up, it's not so bad. But when I'm sitting, it's hard to get up.

I'm still having daily shots to improve the white blood cell counts and every two weeks for the red blood cell counts. It's working, so I'm able to get both taxol and carboplatin. I only have two more chemo sessions, and then I'll have a PET scan in January. Originally, my chemo oncologist said PET scan in December, but

I think he probably doesn't want me thinking about the results over the holidays in case its bad news. If all the cancer is gone, I'll be surprised.

Eventually I come to learn that the doctors never tell you the cancer is gone. They say things like "there is no indication of cancer growing" or "there is no change from the last scan". The reason they caveat the interpretation of the results is because there could always be miniscule traces of cancer that don't easily show up on the scan.

There isn't a day that goes by that I don't feel bad or hurt in some way. I'm wondering how much I'll get back to normal when the chemo stops. If there is still cancer in my body, my chemo oncologist will start the chemo again next year, probably late January. So I guess that's how it goes until I finally say enough. Scan-cancer?-yes?-then chemo, etc. They won't ever do radiation again because they've already caused so much scar tissue that all they have left to radiate is scar tissue. I wish I had the conviction my mom has. She is sure this round of chemo is going to "cure" me totally. With the advancement of my cancer, the fact that surgery was not an option and the prognosis of <5-15% survival after five years, I'm not as convinced as her. Her faith is much stronger than mine.

I am so excited about my new bamboo floor. It looks better than I expected. It makes the whole area look larger and more contiguous. It's funny though, the dogs don't care for it. They huddle up on the few area rugs I've placed around. Scottey won't eat his pig's ear on the floor-he'll go all the way upstairs and eat on the carpet.

The quarter round was finally installed yesterday, completing the flooring job. The dogs are scratching the floor with their claws. I'm so disappointed. I specifically asked the sales person if that would happen and he said no, bamboo is the hardest wood there is. Liar.

It's been raining almost every day for the past 3-4 weeks. The dogs' paws track in mud and I'm forever wiping their paws and mopping the floor every day. I guess I'm only complaining because of the fatigue and I resent having to get up.

One thing I can wholeheartedly recommend if you can afford it or insurance will pay, is to see a psychologist. There was so much going on in my life, with my body, family, co-workers, etc., that I couldn't process it. My psychologist literally saved my life, both mentally and physically. Obviously, I'm still thinking about and grateful to her.

I started lifting weights again about two weeks ago. My upper body is scrawnier than my lower body and I want to build up my upper body muscles. By next summer, I want to be mowing the lawn and working out in the yard and garden again. I also started walking on the treadmill, only walking 15-20 minutes, but it's got to help and can't hurt.

December 14: I got sick again yesterday. I was having lunch with another friend of mine and started getting the chills and shakes. So I ordered a cup of hot chocolate, finished visiting with my friend and resigned myself to going to the clinic. When I got there, the shakes stopped and my fever was 102.5. They started me on IV anti-biotic. Before long came the second round of shakes and chills. The interesting phenomenon about the shakes is that the muscles contract tightly, then loosen, then tighten, then loosen, etc. By the time it all stops (1-2 hours), every muscle in your body aches. I was very dizzy during all this. They had to wheelchair me to get the chest x-ray. I've had a cough for about three weeks now and yesterday couldn't take a breath without coughing. I finally got home from the clinic around 4:30, laid on the couch; fell asleep, climbed into bed. But at least I didn't have to go to prison (hospital). I told my chemo oncologist I absolutely did not want to be admitted into the hospital. So until they have identified the exact strain of the infection, I'll have to go in every day for IV antibiotics. This means I probably won't get my last chemo treatment on Thursday.

December 16: Today I went back for another round of IV antibiotics. When I got home there was a message from the clinic that the preliminary results from yesterday's blood culture was gram negative indicating a blood infection (Klebsiella) the same as last time when I was hospitalized for six days. All this hospital language can sure be confusing. And where the heck did I get the infection this time??

Again, I've been having Leukine or Neupogen shots almost daily to improve my white cell counts. Yesterday it was 6.7 compared to .4 from last Thursday. But starting last week, the shots have caused a serious itching reaction. My chemo oncologist wasn't concerned about it.

You know, I don't recall being advised about the consequences of the damage to the cells from chemo and that it would require having white and red blood cell shots. They're painful and I'm tired of them. But recollection is something we're told chemo can quite destroy.

It's been snowing for the past two days. But since we haven't had any previous freezing days, the ground wasn't cold enough to allow accumulation. Fortunately, I live alone and don't need to get out of the house, so I don't need to shovel the driveway. Four wheel drive, yeah!

I'm getting so excited about going home for Christmas. Uncle Tom called Sunday and he's looking forward to his trip too.

My son, Ash, called Sunday and he'll be arriving in California the same day as me. I'm so looking forward to seeing him, Amy and Elizabeth again.

December 1: The port is going to be taken out Tuesday morning. My chemo oncologist thinks the source of the infections I've had might be the port. I'll be happy to have it out. It's uncomfortable to sleep with and painful sometimes.

My chemo oncologist said they'll only apply a local to pull it out and it'll be easy. Just the thought of it makes me queasy because the port has a tube that extends into my veins.

He also said he would read the PET tomorrow and review it with me. Too cool; can't wait.

And he approved my trip to California next week and my returning to work in January.

December 17: I could not believe it. I fully expected there to be a couple of "suspicious" areas, but my chemo oncologist said there is no evidence of any active cancer growing. The PET won't pick up anything smaller than a pea, so there is a chance it could come back and we just can't see it yet. But for now, I'm reveling in the knowledge that I am free of cancer, no more treatments, shots, pain, fatigue, etc., etc., etc.

I have a huge fever blister (yet again!) that extends from my nose to the top of my lip. Without a doubt, the largest I've ever had. The family is having our portrait taken on the 23rd. The fever blister should be a really nice bright red by then. Hopefully, the picture can be digitally enhanced.

I received a gift from the project managers at work for Christmas and they don't even work for me anymore. They gave me a set of Wursthof knives from Crate n Barrel. What a perfect gift since I love to cook so much. Now I just have to be careful not to cut myself.

Two more days of antibiotics, then the port comes out, and then I'm free of all that crap.

December 20: I went to the hospital to have the port taken out. They didn't use anesthesia, but a local to have the procedure done and therefore I didn't need to arrange a ride home. The same doctor that installed the port removed the port. He was so kind and gracious; he tried to distract me as he removed the port by asking me if I follow basketball. I remember thinking I'm a chick, no way do I follow basketball, then realized that his motive was to distract me, and then started bracing for what was about to come. I still felt it, the pulling of the tube from my stomach, then from my chest. They let me rest for about half an hour and then I felt okay to drive home. And oh, what a freeing feeling that was!!! The last remaining connection between me and the cancer treatments was removed. And I knew I would sleep like a baby that night. And I did.

CHRISTIAN RELIEF:

The man whispered, "God, talk to me" and a parakeet sang. But, the man did not hear.

So the man yelled, "God, talk to me!" And, the thunder rolled across the sky. But, the man did not listen. That night, the man looked around and said, "God let me see you." And a star shined brightly. But the man did not notice. And the man shouted, "God show me a miracle!" And, a life was born. But, the man did not know. So, the man cried out in despair, "Touch me God, and let me know you are here!" Whereupon, God reached down and touched the man. But, the man brushed the butterfly away and walked on. Don't miss out on a blessing because it isn't packaged the way that you expect it to be.

CHAPTER 13

Going Back to Work

DECEMBER 30: I had a wonderful time in California. The time just flew by.

Amy and Ashley gave me a scrapbook of Elizabeth, my beautiful one year old granddaughter, and the scrapbook is absolutely gorgeous. Amy did a really good job on it.

While in California on Monday of this week, a very strange thing happened. My stomach started hurting and within 15 minutes the pain was excruciating. Mom and Dad took me to Urgent Care, who recommended I go to the cancer clinic, who recommended I go to the Emergency Room at the hospital. By now my stomach has been hurting for about 3 hours. I'm sitting there waiting to be seen by the ER doc and literally from one second to the next, the pain disappeared. I got dressed and we went home. Today I went to CICC and told an oncologist (my chemo oncologist, Dr. Logie was on vacation) about the episode. She speculated it would have been gas or bacteria build-up. Oh well. I think it was a by-product of all the treatments, surgeries, blood shots, radiation and other things happening to my body, and maybe withdrawal of all those things! Thankfully, it never happened again.

January 4: I've been back to work for two days now and absolutely no problems. My stamina is good and I seem to have sufficient energy.

We've had rain for 18,000 days in a row now and more is expected tonight.

I'm going back to work!

I met with my new boss today to learn what he wants me to do in my new position as Staff to Executive VP. It sounds like a lot of "providing insight on the folks at Indy" and being a sounding board. He's being careful not to unduly tax me and has asked that I let him know if I get overloaded. He seems very logical and sensitive. He's also indicated that this is only temporary until I'm ready to continue my career path. What he was really telling me was that I'm extraneous and I need to find a new job somewhere.

January 7: I worked 9 hour days this week and even went in on my Friday off for 3 hours. I told the assistant manager to the VPGM that I'm bored and need more responsibilities.

My partial disability ran out in November and I've used all my PTO, so I had no income in December. My HR manager was able to get me approved to be paid for the month even though I didn't work. That was very thoughtful of him. I received a paycheck for the month of December. It's called catastrophic PTO, which I used last year for my treatment appointments. That kind of reinforces the significance of my health situation as catastrophic.

I tried to cash in 500 shares of stock and found out they had been cancelled. It was 500 of the 1500 shares given to me for receiving the CEO award last year. They said the shares were cancelled because I went on medical leave. The HR manager is going to fight it for me. I had planned on using that money to pay for the floor and counter. But counter-intuitively, when you're on medical leave, isn't that when you really need all the money you can get???

January 11: I went to Central Indiana Cancer Center when I got back from California to document the stomach pain I had experienced during my visit to California. I waited 1 ½ hours before I finally saw a substitute chemo oncologist. So to occupy my time, I grabbed my folder from the window outside the room and started reading my medical folder. Several pages referenced my current history labeling me as Stage IV, confirming my fears.

Also, my chemo oncologist said he thought my right index finger going cold was because of the cancer. However, since mid-December, the index finger on my left hand has now gone cold. What up? I'm beginning to wonder if my chemo oncologist thinks my chances are slim.

I've been working 9-10 hours each day and am surprised I have this kind of energy. I recall when I was going through the treatments if I could force myself to get up and do something the fatigue would be mitigated. It would seem that theory still applies.

I've had diarrhea for a month. My big toes are still numb. I have a pain in my back that really hurts. My eyebrows fell out since my last chemo. People at work tell me how great I look. I can't help but think, "If you could only see me without my wig and makeup". They'd be so shocked. People don't really want to see and understand cancer because there is absolutely nothing they can do except empathize.

What the cancer treatments do to people is demeaning and demoralizing. It made me feel like I wasn't equal to other people, like I wasn't quite human.

When I was told in December the PET scan showed no active cancer, my first thought was "I'm a real person again, not something less than a person". I hadn't realized how beaten down I thought I was, like I didn't have the right to feel like a real, whole person. It was like I was "subservient" to others. Then after the scan, I thought "I'm no longer a cancer patient-I'm a cancer survivor." What a liberating feeling that was.

January 13: Today I had to go to the doctor for a severe pain in my back. The pain is close to my right shoulder blade. I couldn't sleep at all last night. It hurt badly all day. It hurts to take a breath. I saw my substitute chemo oncologist at CICC. She wasn't sure what was causing the pain, but ordered a CT scan ASAP. I went directly to Community North and had the CT scan. I didn't realize it but she ordered a CT of my chest and abdomen, so I had to drink that barium crap. If it's serious I know they'll call me right away. If it's not serious, I have an appointment to see Dr. Logie on Monday and I'll find out then.

Yesterday, it was 68 degrees. Today it's snowing and expected to be cold for the next 4-5 days. Yeah! I hate the cold.

The President of our business unit was in Indy today and came by my office to see me. He used to be the VPGM here in Indy and had a high regard for my capabilities and reputation. He was the one I shared a table with when I received the CEO award. He was so considerate and advised me not to work long hours and he's right. I have a 5-15% (what the heck, it varies depending upon the source of information and so varies here in my book!) chance of survival after five years. I need to consider how I want to spend the next five years in case I'm in the 85-95% that doesn't make it.

I'm thinking if my cancer recurs in the near term, my chances of survival are slim. If it doesn't come back after 1-2 years, I may have a chance.

I really don't understand. I quit smoking 10 years ago. If my lungs are clean after seven years, how did I get cancer?

January 19: I saw my chemo oncologist on Monday and confronted him about my folder stating I am Stage IV. He didn't offer an apology or reason why he misled me, but I am Stage IV. I asked him if Stage IV is terminal and he tap danced. I went to WebMD and it stated a 15-35% survival after a year. And <2% chance of survival after five years. I figure I was diagnosed in July and its now January so I've survived seven months into my first year. A good friend and mentor of mine (the cook of the infamous Thanksgiving dinner) Karen gave me good advice=live your life normally, do the things you want to/would normally do. I'm going to finish my Master's degree. It's very important to me. I would be the first one in our family to get a Masters. Someone needs to blaze the trail!

I'm enjoying my job. I'd like to spend more time with my boss, the new VPGM, to learn from him. He is so bright. I'm working 9-10 hours/day and still have energy when I get home. It's so great to have energy again. I've never been the kind of person to sit around, but have always needed to be up and doing things physically.

I'm going to live like there is nothing wrong, unless and until cancer shows up again. I told my chemo oncologist above all else I want honesty. I have decisions to make. I also told him I can do another round of chemo, but not sure how many more rounds after that. There's got to be a tradeoff between chemo/survival and living out the remainder of life with some sort of quality.

My chemo oncologist said my chance of the cancer recurring was "substantial". I'd expected a recurrence, but only one.

Tomorrow night, a bunch of us are going out for dinner and drinks. It'll be good to get out and socialize like a normal person.

It got down to negative 5 degrees last night. I hate the cold. We've had a lot of snow already this winter and this weekend, and we're supposed to get a lot more.

Saturday, I'm getting a body massage. And Sunday is the annual meeting at Holy Family Church.

My diarrhea is finally gone after five weeks. I'm sure I wasn't eating the appropriate foods that make the diarrhea subside. Three toes on each foot are still "asleep". Both index fingers on each hand have little circulation and are very cold all the time. It's very uncomfortable. The only time they're warm is when I'm asleep. My chemo oncologist said absolutely no surgery. Why didn't I ask him "why" (SEE THE TREND?) What a recurring question. I was so good about making a list of questions for my weekly oncologist visits, but rarely have the courage to question the doctor's statements. It's probably that perspective that doctors are obviously well educated and who am I to question what he says?

January 27: Well, my job up until now was comfortable. Then the VPGM (Vice President General Manger) asked me to manage the F-15 spares project. It is a program that is high maintenance, high pressure and high visibility and also very overrun to the tune of millions of dollars. It's going to consume about ½ my day and I'm concerned that I'll be able to do enough to make any kind of positive improvement since the problem has been building for almost two years.

I wish I could find Teresa, my high school friend. She was my best friend in high school and I'd really like to talk to her about my condition.

I have little baby eyelashes coming out. My eyebrows came back first and they're very dark, black. No hair on my head yet; it's still peach fuzz.

I so hate the cold. Both my index fingers are always cold. The only time they're warm is when I'm sleeping and what good does that do me. How much longer is this Reynaud's syndrome going to continue??? I was hoping that maybe when the treatments stopped and the cancer stopped growing the Reynaud's would also go away.

February 1: I've been back to work for a month now. I'm still working 9-10 hours per day and having no adverse effects.

This F-15 program is 1 ½ years into a 3 year contract, so I'm not sure how much I can improve it, but I'll sure try.

There is an open requisition for a Director position in Long Beach, California which would be a promotion. I haven't applied for it because 1) it required a Master's degree, which I don't have yet and 2) I'm not sure how much longer I have to live.

Tomorrow I'm going to the Program Leadership Forum for my company. It was at this forum last year that I was given the 2003 Program Leadership Award.

February 8: The Leadership Forum was okay. Some speakers were good, others not as much.

My friend, Bill, came by the facility today. He's survived the prognosis of his doctor. He's now trying to get approved at the Bethesda National Institute of Health for a clinical trial for a bone marrow transplant. His prognosis was 7-9 months and he's surpassed that by about 6 months so far. Saturday, we're going out for lunch. It's nice to talk to someone you know who's been through the same hell.

I live in fear every day that the cancer will come back. I keep looking for signs, but there are none.

The "sleepiness" in my toes/feet is diminishing. But when I walk on the treadmill, I get a tingly feeling in my legs.

I've been working out on the treadmill, trying to work up to 25 minutes of fast walking. I'm about ½ way there. My goal is to be running outside by this summer.

I should be re-joining the Master's Program on April 10. There will be too much on my plate by then – the Master's Program, managing the F-15 program, Executive staff to VP, and the final prep for the Logistics Conference I've been organizing. I'm excited about the conference-it'll be the first ever for the aerospace company I work for and we have some high level speakers, which are drawing a lot of attendees. My co-worker, Lynn, has been helping me and doing a terrific job. She's really good. I'm getting excited about it.

This conference is my brain-child. I'm trying to get the company to come together on our common logistics needs. The conference ends up running for four years, until they decide it's getting too big and needs to be assigned to a VP, who ends up not having enough time to make it happen. No one else wants to tackle this big job, so it ends up falling to the wayside. It's like watching your project turn to dust, knowing in your heart there is a problem and this is the solution.

COMIC RELIEF:

Sister Mary entered the Monastery of Silence. The Priest said, "Sister, this is a silent monastery. You are welcome here as long as you like, but you may not speak until I direct you to do so..."

Sister Mary lived in the monastery for 10 years before the Priest said to her, "Sister Mary, you have been here for 10 years. You can speak two words." Sister Mary said, "Hard bed."

"I'm sorry to hear that," the Priest said, "We will get you a better bed..."

After another 10 years, Sister Mary was called by the Priest... "You may say another two words, Sister Mary."

"Cold food," said Sister Mary, and the Priest assured her that the food would be better in the future...

On her 30th anniversary at the monastery, the Priest again called Sister Mary into his office.

"Two words you may say today."

"I quit," said Sister Mary.

"It is probably best", said the Priest, "You've done nothing but complain since you got here."

CHAPTER 14

The First Scan After the First Scan

FEBRUARY 18: I saw my chemo oncologist yesterday. I am scheduled for a CT scan on March 3, and then see my oncologist on March 17, with a chest x-ray. During the appointment yesterday, he asked when my last PET was. He looked in his file and commented "marked improvement" as the result of the PET. That sure sounds different from "you're clean". Also, I asked about long term disability and he said something like "you do have lung cancer". It tears me up going in there. I live each day thinking I am almost a normal person. Then I get a kind of reality check that the cancer will likely come back. It's very confusing. Do I make long/short term plans? How much time do I have before it comes back?

Should I try to finish the Master's program? Should I quit my job? Should I reduce the responsibility of my job? Should I quit working out?

I apply for long term disability every year after my diagnosis for five years and am denied each year due to a "pre-existing condition". I never applied for long term disability because I always thought that I've always been so healthy, rarely getting a cold even; thinking I'll never have a life threatening disease.

I am so sick about this refinanced loan I have with Chevy Chase. I've been so screwed. A 3% pre-payment penalty. It's an ARM and I thought it was fixed, the principal can go up and the interest rate can go as high as 19.9%. I'm going to see my lawyer. I signed these papers in September when I was sick, and definitely, the loan officer did not explain all this to me. And to my dismay, I should not have signed any legal documents in my condition.

On Tuesday, it was 68 degrees, and then it snowed that night. Go figure.

February 28: Can't believe how fast time is flying. I'm working 10-11 hours/day. Now John has scheduled a meeting for Saturday 1-4pm. Not exactly adhering to my company president's advice to take it easy!

All next week I'll be in Boston for a Principles of Program Leadership Course. I've heard the food is outrageous and everyone gains weight. I don't need that. I'm finally up to my normal weight and then some . . .

I'm working out almost every day. 25 minutes walking very fast on the treadmill; although I haven't tried running yet.

I'm getting a bonus this week. I'm grateful to get anything since I wasn't at work for four months last year. $23,000. I'll need that if I have to take time off work for treatments.

I have a CT scan scheduled for Thursday, but won't get the results until my appointment with my chemo oncologist on March 17.

We're getting a couple inches of snow tonight. I hate the cold. By the end of April, the chance of snow is pretty much gone. I'm so looking forward to a warm house with the windows open.

My master's program starts up April 10th. I'm anxious to complete this. Although it's going to be tough trying to remember what I learned in the previous classes since they all build on each other.

March 15: I have appointments with both my chemo oncologist and Dr. Hardacre on Thursday. One of them will tell me the results of the CT scan I had on March 3. I'm nervous. I want more time before they tell me it's back. The more time between the treatments and the re-occurrence, the better. I really, really want to complete my Master's program.

The weather is really trying to turn into spring. I'm so looking forward to warm weather and being able to be outside. I really want to resume doing the yard work.

Not sure why I'm so depressed tonight. I know I'm working a lot of hours and the troubled program I'm working on is very stressful and I'm always in some kind of pain. My back has hurt from my shoulders to my lower back for two months now to the point where it hurts to stand/sit/bend over and put on socks.

Both my index fingers are always cold.

I'm gaining weight like crazy. I'm up to 110 pounds, which is about 5 pounds over normal.

I've noticed I'm more tired lately.

I'm so tired of this. I look at other people and envy how they don't have pain every day and can work all day and still feel good. It's been a year since I've been that way.

I have battle scars all over my nose and upper lip from the fever blisters last year.

I don't have enough hair to go without the wig and the wig is so uncomfortable and unnatural.

My left hand has hurt for at least six months. Not sure if its muscle or ligament or??

My toes have been asleep or numb for three months. I can feel things, but they feel asleep.

I'm finally working out on the treadmill almost every day walking fast for 25 minutes. I've tried running, but can only run for 2-3 minutes at a time. Just can't seem to get my breath. And I'm too tired, must be all the radiation burn on my chest.

March 17: Saw Drs' Logie and Hardacre today. Dr. Hardacre had the CT scans up and went over them with me. I'm still clean. In fact there has been a decrease in the size of the lymph nodes, plus much scar tissue. I don't have to go back for three months!!!

The first thing I did was to thank God. Then I called Mom and Dad. Again, it's funny, kids are always your kids. Ash will always be my baby. And as old as I am, I am still my parents' child. My mom wouldn't go anywhere today so she wouldn't miss my call. She and Dad have been my rock and my support system.

COMIC RELIEF:

A guy is driving around the back woods of Montana and he sees a sign in front of a broken down shanty-style house: 'Talking Dog for Sale' He rings the bell and the owner appears and tells him the dog is in the backyard. The guy goes into the backyard and sees a nice looking Labrador retriever sitting there. 'You talk?' he asks . . . 'Yep,' the Lab replies. After the guy recovers from the shock of hearing a dog talk, he says 'So, what's your story?' The Lab looks up and says, 'Well, I discovered that I could talk when I was pretty young. I wanted to help the government, so I told the CIA. In no time at all they had me jetting from country to country, sitting in rooms with spies and world leaders, because no one figured a dog would be eaves dropping.' 'I was one of their most valuable spies for eight years running. But the jetting around really tired me out, and I knew I wasn't getting any younger so I decided to settle down. I signed up for a job at the airport to do some undercover security, wandering near suspicious characters and listening in. I uncovered some incredible dealings and was awarded a batch of medals.' 'I got married, had a mess of puppies, and now I'm just retired.' The guy is amazed. He goes back in and asks the owner what he wants for the dog. 'Ten dollars,' the guy says. 'Ten dollars? This dog is amazing! Why on earth are you selling him so cheap?' 'Because he's a liar. He never did any of that stuff.

CHAPTER 15

And so it Begins

MARCH 18: ONLY had to work two hours today to complete my 40 hours for the week, but John had meetings scheduled for my team until 6:00 pm, so that put me at about 10 hours overtime for the week.

I told Karen (the Controller who had prepared our infamous, enjoyable and memorable Thanksgiving dinner) that I had a clean CT scan and she started to cry. I was a little surprised and uncomfortable. She jumped up and gave me a hug. Then she asked if I'd told John (our VPGM and he was standing close by) so I had to tell him. I just don't think he wants to get close to anyone. He just wants to do his job and not get involved.

I don't have to go back for three months for a scan so I can get almost ½ way through the Master's program. Then if the cancer comes back, I should still be able to complete the program. It is so important to me to get that Masters. I'd be the first in our family to obtain a Master's degree. One leads to two, then three, four, etc., and we become an educated family.

March 20: Just got home from the trip from hell. Me and my project manager travelled to California on a business trip on Monday. The first plane was late arriving in St. Louis so we missed the second plan. We ran from our landing gate to the departing gate but missed it by a couple of minutes. My chest was about to explode from the running. I ended up walking then running, then walking, running. We landed in California around midnight. Today on our day to return home, I woke up at the hotel and had no hot water so I couldn't take a shower.

Then I got an email from one of our VPs scheduling a 5:00 pm meeting on my Friday off. I haven't had a Friday off since I got back to work in January. So my President warned me previously to take it easy and not over-do it at work and I never heeded his advice, but caved to the pressure of others that report to him.

Then, I got to National Car Rental to return the car and realized they overcharged me. And, in the National Shuttle to the airport, the bus driver was compelled to talk to me the entire time about her personal hygiene. Then I get to the airport and standing in the security line, some agent rudely pulled me out of line and told me I had too many carry-ons. I had a small pocketbook, a briefcase and a small roll-on suitcase. I put my pocketbook in the suitcase and whallah, I'm now compliant! So what was the freaking deal?

I get to the kennel to pick up my dogs about 5:40 (they close at 6:00) and guess what . . . they closed at 4:00 for inventory. They let me in anyway probably since I've given them so darned much money and they saw the haggard look on my face.

And just to put the icing on the cake, the guy I was travelling with works for me and HE had first class tickets the whole way!!

It was 78 degrees here in Indy when I got home today. It's supposed to get down to 50 degrees and rainy through the weekend.

I called my sister, Liz, on Wednesday and just broke down. I didn't realize how much all of this hit home. I'm so afraid, trying to be brave.

I still don't have enough hair to go without a wig. I hate the wig. It hurts and it itches.

I'm back in the Master's program. Just have to stay clean long enough to finish this. This new class has been very kind and welcoming. Tomorrow, I'm meeting with one of the guys in the class to talk. He offered. I've received several welcoming emails. Have to wonder what they've been told about me joining in the middle of their program. Three of the five classes are the same as last year. In June, we go to Amsterdam and to Paris in September.

This weekend is going to be beautiful weather; sunny and 70 degrees. Yes!! I love it.

I still can't run. I'm walking very fast on the treadmill but can only run 2-3 minutes. My goal was to run by this summer.

My back hurts all the time and I've had 2-3 body massages since December, but they don't help. In fact, the last one hurt badly. So maybe it's not muscle?

My left hand has hurt for about three months. I've been wearing a brace hoping that would help.

My toes are still asleep.

My index fingers are still always ice cold. The only time they are warm is when I lay down. Can't figure out how being prone can make my fingers get warm.

The grass is turning green; the leaves are coming out on the bushes and trees. The daffodils are blooming. I love it. I'm debating whether or not to mow the grass. BECAUSE I CAN!! A new beginning!

April 12: I've signed up for some sort of Aids or Cancer run/walk for the past 15-20 years. This year when I filled out the form I indicated "cancer survivor". When I got my packet today, everything was "pink" – the tee shirt, cap, boa, ribbon for car and invitation to participate in the survivors parade. I cried. At the walk, they had everyone line up and start the race according to how long they had survived. They started with 50 years and there were about a half dozen women. I was so surprised because 50 years ago, they didn't have the medications and treatments they do today. Then, they went to 40, 30, 20, 10, 5, 1 and less than one. There were very few people walking with me in the "less than one year" category, but it was rewarding all the same.

I've done a lot of crying this past week and a half or so. Last week, I found out a friend of mine at work, her cancer is back with a vengeance. Monday, some of us got together and put together a nice basket of gifts for her and I agreed to bring it to her. I called her tonight and told her I'd like to bring the gift basket to her Friday. I've felt such a kindred spirit with her.

I haven't told my project manager, Bill, about our other mutual friend of ours, Cindy, at work because he's going through so much right now with his stem cell transplant and chemo. He doesn't need to know/worry about someone who's been clean for two years and now has stage IV lymph node, lung and liver cancer.

I want to be the creator of the 1st annual Enterprise Logistics Solutions Conference. It is scheduled for May 17-19. I'm so excited. All the speakers are lined up. We have 80 people registered. It's finally becoming a reality.

In my career with this company I have discovered a disconnect between the six different business units of the company. We are very autonomous from each other. Each business independently creates their own programs, spreadsheets, and solutions for our customers. If we come together, we can share what we've created/learned and save the customer so much money.

There is something in my neck that hurts. If I move a certain way, the pain connects to my back. The back pain started about 3-4 months ago. But my last CT scan on my chest was clean. I never know when to start worrying, unless of course the pain is extreme.

April 14: Tomorrow, I'm taking a huge basket to our friend, Cindy. She only lives about 7 miles from me. I'm going to study in the morning then go to her house. She had her first chemo today.

This weekend is going to be really nice and in the 70's. I'm going to mow the lawn for the first time. It's getting pretty high. I so enjoy being outside and working on the yard. The first couple of times I get out there and try to start the mower, it's difficult and I have to keep pulling on the cable. I'm embarrassed that I can't get the mower started.

I'm a little bit ahead of the curve in the Master's program for this final module. Two thirds of the classes are the same as last year and the readings and homework assignment are roughly the same. Last year, I'd gotten through all the assignments and was ready for the 1st in-residency when I was diagnosed. It's been almost a year since then. I went through so much last year. Weekly chemo, radiation, 4 surgeries, 2 hospitalizations, almost died, very serious stuff. And today I feel almost normal.

The hair on the top of my head is about ½" long and the hair on the back of my head is about 1" long. Still not long enough to go without a wig. At this rate, it'll be fall before I can lose the wig. Cindy will be losing her hair in 2-4 weeks. I'm going to offer to her that we can go somewhere bald together to make her more comfortable. Her doctor has decided to increase the number of chemo drugs from 1 to 3 each week. That doesn't sound good.

She said the installation of her port was no big deal and she was fine the next day. Why did mine hurt so much?

April 18: I participated in the Race for the Cure on Saturday. It was kind of weird wearing the pink T shirt, BOA and medal. 161 people at Raytheon signed up. It was the largest sign up ever. I counted 27,500 white T shirts so there must have been about 40,000 people there. The largest number pink T shirt (survivor) I saw was 1726. I brought Scottey with me. He's done the walk with me almost every year since I've been here.

On Sunday, Holy Family had a baby shower for Reverend Kristi. It was kind of surreal because I really haven't spent any time with the women of the church other than Sunday services; haven't been well enough to get involved. She received a ton of gifts. It was so neat because we don't pay her very much.

So often, I think about cancer and it coming back. I try so hard to be positive and happy. Meanwhile, I have all these aches and pains. My hair still isn't long enough to go without a wig so when can I feel normal??

I talk to Bill twice/week. He calls me around Wednesday and I call him on the weekends. The clinical trial (stem cell transplant) is going well. He thinks he may be able to go home in a couple of weeks. I don't know what options he has if this doesn't work. His doctors already told him there is no more chemo that can work.

April 21: Tomorrow is Michael's birthday (my brother). 40 years old. Monday is my 50 year birthday.

I'm taking tomorrow off to get ahead on homework. Weather's going to suck so I won't feel compelled to be outside. It's been in the 70s & 80s and now this weekend-a chance of snow!!

On my birthday, I have two major presentations, I hate presentations.

I talked to Bill tonight. He's doing well. His neutrophil count has to be 50 degrees before he's released from the hospital. It's currently at 260. His transplant was 2 ½ weeks ago and it took that long to get to 260.

And another different friend had a complete mastectomy a couple weeks ago. She tested positive for the breast cancer gene with an 87% likelihood of getting breast cancer. The mastectomy was preventative.

I had my eyes checked today. My prescription has only changed slightly. I picked out new glasses, they're frameless. So the mailbox and curb incidents were only temporary!

I talked to Mom tonight. Dad's back is so much better. He's been having problems with a lot of pain in his back. We were all convinced that the recliner he had was causing the problem. It was tilted to one side! Finally he got rid of it. She said today his hands hurt from lifting bricks. He's going to be 75 this year. What a milestone!

April 24: Took Friday off to get homework done and I did, but also ended up doing 4-5 hours of work. I just give away too much time to work. I went to the dentist on Friday. Extremely panicky because they laid me down and put my head lower than my feet. This causes choking in my throat, so we had to take it slow.

I had the oil changed on the BMW thinking that the oil needed to be changed at 5,000 miles. I bought this BMW last year anticipating my graduation with an MBA last year, so now it's an early graduation present. After they completed the oil change, the guy told me it's not necessary to do so until every 8-10,000 miles. It didn't even occur to me to challenge him why he didn't tell me that before he conducted the oil change and charged me!! And why didn't I check the manual to know how often to change the oil? (AGAIN DIDN'T ASK!)

April 29: Finally took a 9/80 Friday off-sort of. Worked at home for about 3 hours, and then did homework for about 3 hours. After doing the running around, I did the yard work in the front yard. While I was sweeping the driveway, a neighbor lady came over and apologized for not coming over sooner. Said she was a nurse and noticed I was having trouble with some sort of sickness and offered whatever help I might need. I was so surprised, but come on, all winter long you noticed and couldn't come talk to me?

I'm still so conscientious of not having hair. When is it ever going to grow out?

It's been gray and overcast, and now been raining for two weeks.

CHRISTIAN RELIEF:

The children were lined up in the cafeteria of a Catholic school for lunch. At the head of the table was a large pile of apples. The nun made a note, "Take only one, God is watching."

Moving through the line, to the other end of the table, was a large pile of chocolate chip cookies. One of the boys wrote a note, "Take all you want, God is watching the apples."

CHAPTER 16

The Long Road to Recovery

MY VP LET me know that I'm being considered for a position "to run an organization" in California. I'd love to get back to warm weather and family, but am concerned about leaving my oncologists. They have both been so good. So far I'm still clean. They have prescribed all the chemo and radiation I could stand and so far it seems to have worked.

I've lost my lower eye lashes again-those were the first to grow back and now they're gone again. What's up?

My 50th birthday was Monday. Thankfully, nothing eventful happened-like trashing my office. I did receive a bouquet of flowers from Mom & Dad.

My baby sister, Liz, sent me an extremely touching letter about how much she admired me, all I've been through and all I've accomplished. I cried. I was so touched.

The pain in my right shoulder hasn't gone away since January. Tonight it hurts particularly badly.

The numbness in my toes is still there, but seems to be receding.

Deb Carver asked me the other day if I was seeing anyone. She had someone she wanted to introduce to me. How odd. 50 years old and cancer. I told her I'd think about it – that I had had cancer and didn't think it was fair to get involved with anyone.

Somehow in the past two months I've gained so much weight I can't fit into my suits. I've got to lose some weight. Remember when previously I talked about how I had my suits taken in because I'd lost so much weight? What a waste of time and money! How silly to think I'd stay at that weight, while eating crazily. I've been walking on the treadmill almost every day (and running for four minutes). I'd be even heavier if I hadn't been working out every day.

Last Thursday, I briefed Bryan Even (our business unit President) and Sue B (our new Deputy GM) on a spares program, and then also discussed this new position with my new boss and his HR Director.

After reviewing the materials my new potential boss gave me, I was excited about the things I'd like to do with this organization. Today, I told John and my HR director that I'd like to accept the offer. The relocation package will cover all my expenses and I should get a small increase in salary.

The conference I created is next week. I'll be so glad when it's over. So many details, so much to coordinate.

The weather is terrific, finally. It was 82 degrees today and thunderstorms expected this evening. Thunderstorms and tornadoes are normal this time of year.

May 20: I'm in a de-compressing mode. The 1st Annual Enterprise Logistics Conference was held May 17-19 at the Omni Hotel. I MC'd the whole thing which was very stressful. We had 150 people the first day and only about 75 people the second day, which is normal. Most folks come for the high-drawing speakers on the first day, then go home the next day. General Stalder (USMC) spoke on the first day and he was awesome, acked with insight.

On the second day, we had Scott Cronk who talked about the teamwork required in the Indy 500 race and its related pit stops. Indianapolis, being the one and only Indy-500 annual race location!

A lot of positive feedback (verbally) on the conference . . . whoo-hoo! I spoke with our corporate VP today about my new job and she congratulated me a couple of times on the conference. That is good that corporate views the conference as a success. I wouldn't mind doing it again now that I've learned so much and fortunately, my co-chair, Lynn, enjoyed it and wants to help with the next one. She was incredible. Several people were enthusiastic to meet her. She must have positively answered dozens of emails from these people because they sought her out during the conference to let her know how significantly she had assisted them.

May 23: I told my potential new boss that I'd like to accept the position in Long Beach. When I talked to his VP on Friday, she said they would have to post the job. That tells me it'll be later than August before I get to move. In my mind, the acceptance of the offer is predicated on my next CT scan being negative. The next scan is June 1. But if it takes three months to go through the HR process, I'll be getting another CT scan by then.

I still have so many aches and pains. My back really hurts. Massages haven't helped. In fact, they seem to make it worse.

Both my index fingers are cold all the time. Sometimes, my third and pinkie fingers also turn purple. I never tell people about this, but always try to portray a very positive attitude and act like nothing is wrong. Not a single day goes by that something doesn't hurt.

I lost all my eyelashes again. I don't get it. The chemo stopped in December and yet in May I lose my eyelashes again??? How lucky am I??? The lower lids have come back, now I'm waiting on the upper lids to return. I don't think people notice. At least they don't say anything.

May 31: What an absolutely gorgeous weekend. I took my 9/80 Friday and Monday was Memorial Day, so four days off in a row! And the weather was perfect. I got so much done outside; even managed to get some sunburn. I couldn't let that happen with the chemo last year. I worked in my garden quite a bit. It has been two years since I pruned and trimmed and it sure needed it.

I also got the deck floor restained with redwood. It had worn off so much from the snow and sun it was almost white. That was important if I'm going to sell this place.

I got my first haircut tonight! It's not even long enough to go without a wig yet, but its growing over my ears and sticking out of my wig in the back. Dubbie is so good. It was so good to see her again. She's so considerate, she didn't charge me, yet again.

Another first-I finally started running again on Friday. Did my usual three mile route with the dogs and ran about 2/3 of the three miles and walked really fast in between. Such a milestone! So happy!

I leave on the 12th for Amsterdam for the Master's program. Then I come home on Saturday the 25th and then leave on the 26th for Boston for an Advanced Program Leadership Pilot course I was asked to participate in. We are to evaluate the course as well as attend. My poor dogs will be in the kennel for three weeks in a row, longest they've ever been kenneled.

Somehow this year I've gained 7 pounds. Gee, I wonder if it's all the sweets and desserts! My suits don't fit anymore. I've spent a lot of money on them and sure can't afford to replace them. Now that I'm running again, that will burn some calories and I've been significantly reducing the carbs.

Tomorrow I have my third CT scan since the chemo stopped in December. I feel good, but then I felt good when I was diagnosed. I'm nervous and scared. I don't think I'll ever get used to this, probably just have to deal with it every three months.

My cousin Tim has cancer. See, now I'm made aware of this fact. Apparently it's pretty bad. I haven't heard any news from my mom on how he's doing, which isn't good. I'm almost afraid to ask, just in case.

Cindy is not doing so well. She finally saw her usual oncologist after her last CT scan and he wasn't very optimistic. Her doctor said they'd do chemo for about six months and then "he didn't know".

My friend, Debbie, with the aneurism is scheduled for surgery within a couple of days. It was so strange because the day before her surgery, we are standing there talking about her surgery and her best friend strangely starts backing away from the group, exclaiming that our friend isn't doing good, she was kind of fearful of the surgery. It turns out that her surgery is not successful and our dear friend does not make it. I go to her funeral and am walking around the room beforehand with pictures of her and her family and just lose it. I have to leave to compose myself and don't make it to her funeral. I guess everything I've been through, having three friends enduring their own suffering of cancer and now Debbie succumbing to an aneurism just added up to more than I could take.

Bill is still in Bethesda while they monitor him after his stem cell transplant. He's always so depressed and down. It's hard to talk to him every Friday. Nothing I say encourages him to be more positive and optimistic. I hope I'm doing some good for him.

June 1: Had the CT scan this morning. They have a new drink, instead of the barium shake. It's just two glasses of flavored water (not flavored very well). They had to stick me three times to get a vein. I'll call my chemo oncologist to get the results. Please God.

I saw on TV the other day about a child that was born with cancer. How the hell does that happen? Where is the fairness? I mean, really, an innocent child?

COMIC RELIEF:

A couple is driving through the country having an argument and they pass a bay of pigs. The husband says to the wife "relatives of yours?" She replies, "yes, in-laws".

CHAPTER 17

Moving on Literally and Figuratively

June 2: THANK you God. My chemo oncologist finally called me at 4:45. There have been no changes since the last CT scan. No indication of cancer in the liver or adrenal glands. I have been so anxious about this; I've had diarrhea and an upset stomach for two days. I wish there was some way to get used to this. As I get further away from the last chemo, my chances keep improving. Cindy was Stage I breast cancer, and then clean for two years. Then Stage IV and it's in her liver, lymph nodes, sternum and lungs. I can't help but compare and wonder with what vengeance mine will come back.

For now I'm grateful that I may be moving back to So Cal. I can focus on finishing the Master's program and I'm good to go for the next three months. Thank you, God.

June 5: I realized this weekend I've continued using the incorrect thought process and terminology for a "clean" CT scan. My chemo oncologist keeps saying "there has been no change since the last CT scans" which I translated to "clean CT scan and no cancer". In reality, there could still be cancer but it just isn't growing or showing up on the scan. I'm convinced the chemo has a residual effect-hence the hair is slow to return and my eyelashes fell out twice. Now I'm scared for my hair to grow back-it might mean either the cancer is growing or the chemo has stopped working.

I talked to my potential new boss this week. He said he was trying to have the requisition open this week for the position. I'll apply, and then he'll have to interview people then hopefully tell me I have the job. I want this to be done before my next CT scan in September.

I have to admit I appreciate his compassion. When I asked "what if my cancer comes back"? His reply was "then we'll deal with that if it happens". Too cool.

I really like my house and will really miss the spaciousness. And I love my new kitchen remodel.

I'm finally running every day again, just like before the diagnosis. The dogs and I do our usual two-three mile route and every couple of days I try to run just a little further.

Today it was very humid. Poor dogs had a hard time and when we got home they panted hard for about 45 minutes. Scottey got a little chunky over the winter, as a result of not much exercise due to my predicament.

June 20: I'm in the Netherlands right now. Tilburg to be exact. Today begins week two of the 3.1 In Residency for the MBA program. This week we have Strategic Management and International Negotiations. Last week it was International Management, Stress Management (how appropriate for me at this time!), Rewarding People and Geopolitics. Geopolitics was taught by an Indian woman, in her mid-70s. Extremely knowledgeable. I was thoroughly impressed with her.

It was in the low 60s when I first got here. I wasn't expecting it to be so cold, so I had to call a taxi to take me to the nearest department store to buy a coat. Now it's in the low 80s. Probably because I went out and bought a coat!

In this country, all the landscaping is so intentionally planted and so well kept up.

About 50% of the population uses bicycles for transportation. The government purchases the bicycles and people are free to take them from one place to the next and leave it there. Apparently there are very few thefts of the bicycles. In fact one of the guys in my class doesn't even own a car because so many people prefer the use of the bicycle. And there are very few overweight Dutch people. How on earth would I bring all those groceries home and cart the dogs around and all the trees and plants for the yard? Such a different lifestyle and different culture.

June 21: Seven days down, four to go. This week would appear to be pretty easy. Class gets out around 4:30-5:00 today. Since we had no assignments to work on, I went for a walk, then a swim. Dinner is at 6:30.

I showed up at this In-Residency without my wig. It's just been too hot and it's too uncomfortable. This is me and I can't do anything about it. My hair is at a length (or shortness) that one would think either 1) she's trying to make a fashion statement or 2) she's recently had chemo. I know I wasn't smart enough before I was diagnosed to even know what causes a cancer patient's hair to fall out.

In retrospect, I believe someone must have explained to the class that I would be joining them and that I had had cancer/treatments.

During the end of the In-Residency, we were to take our graduation picture and I put my wig on, wanting to look a little more normal. As a result, several people re-introduced themselves to me. It was just a little too uncomfortable.

I must have overdone the running. My left knee hurts and my left ankle is swollen. It hurts when I walk, so I haven't run since I arrived here. It wakes me up at night sometimes and doesn't seem to be getting any better. The problem is that all we do is sit, eat, and sleep in this program. I need to exercise and get the cobwebs out.

July 4: Finally home from the last In-Residency in the Netherlands. It is our nation's birthday. I'm BBQ'ing chicken. It's probably a sacrilege not to.

I had a PET scan on Thursday and have an appointment with my chemo oncologist on the seventh to get the results. Since I just had a CT scan a month ago and there was no change, I'm fairly confident the PET won't show anything. The tech who did the PET did educate me on PETs and CTs. The CT looks at structure and anatomy, while the PET looks at organs. The CT shows what spots which could be swollen lymph nodes, cancer or scar tissue. The PET shows cancerous activity. The cancer is activated by the glucose injected into the bloodstream before the PET scan is done. The exciting thing is that they are now matching up the CT with its suspicious areas to the PET with the activated cancer to determine almost for certain where active cancer is. The subjectivity of the tests has always been frustrating to me, so this is kind of exciting.

When I told my oncologist that I'm being offered a position in California, he strongly suggested it might not be best for me to move away from Indianapolis. Not sure what the motive was behind that statement, but I knew in my heart it was the best move for me. I would be closer to my family, I would be away from the dreadful cold weather and I would be away from the memories and reminders of the difficult treatment program that thankfully saved me.

The fifth In-Residency for the Master's program is over. Now we have mid-terms throughout July. The last In-Residency is Paris in September, then finals in October and graduate in December. I'm so excited.

There was an email from my favorite Uncle Tom when I got back from Amsterdam. My cousin Tim has died from cancer. I cried. Today I sent an email to my aunt Margaret, his mom. She took it really rough. I just wanted her to know how much it meant to me to have family around when I was so sick, just to let her know that her being there for Tim had to have been the most important thing to him.

My folks didn't tell me about him dying, perhaps in order to protect me from the sadness associated with cancer or maybe to prevent me from thinking about my own vulnerability. Who gets such great parents?

August 12: I have another CT scan.

August 14: An appointment with my new oncologist in Long Beach to go over the results of the last scan. I have a spot on my lungs and one on my sternum. He says its slow growing, so we'll wait until November and do another scan to see how fast it is growing. I cry all the way home. My sister, Liz, calls to get the results and I couldn't talk for several seconds, and then told her the cancer is back. She was so positive and encouraging; it really made me feel better immediately.

I found a website that will locate lost friends for a nominal fee. I pay with my credit card and plug in my friend Teresa's information and after a few seconds, a list of her most recent addresses is displayed. I call information for the last address and magically I am given her phone number. I call and we are both surprised to connect with each other again. I know I cried when I heard her voice and cried again after we hung up. I've known this woman since high school (30 years) and we lost touch when she moved within Georgia at the same time I moved from Long Beach, CA to Indianapolis, IN. We've kept in touch ever since. And now that we're in our late 50's, our conversations consist mostly of comparing old-peoples' ailments!

COMIC RELIEF:

The wedding day was fast approaching. Everything was ready, and nothing could dampen Debbie's excitement, not even her parents' nasty divorce. Her mother, Dorris, had found the PERFECT dress to wear and would be the best dressed mother-of-the-bride EVER! A week later, Debbie was horrified to learn her father's new young wife, Barb, had purchased the exact same dress! She asked Barb to exchange the dress, but Barb refused. "Absolutely not! I'm wearing this dress. I look like a million bucks in it!" Debbie told her mother, who graciously replied, "Never mind, Sweetheart, I'll get another dress. After all, it's YOUR special day." Two weeks later Debbie and her mother went shopping and found another awesome dress. When they stopped for lunch, Debbie asked her mother, "What are you going to do with the first dress? Maybe you should return it. You really don't have any place to wear it." Dorris grinned and replied, "Of course, I do, Dear! I'm wearing it to the rehearsal dinner!"

CHAPTER 18

New Beginnings

AUGUST 28: TODAY is the first day of my new job in California as Director of a business unit. Another new beginning.

To get to this point, there is a long process of interviewing all the candidates and finally it is determined I am the best candidate.

Then driving into work on my first day, I get a call on my cell phone from my friend's wife who tells me Bill has passed from his stomach cancer. He was told initially there was nothing they could do. He made them do surgery to remove the tumor. Then he tried the stem cell transplant. I called him just about every week to check in on him. Towards the end, I now realize he was failing the fight. He was so very doped up on morphine, I could barely understand him. I just kept thinking he'd get better.

September is the FINAL In-Residency in Paris. I'm so absolutely excited to be visiting this country. It has always been my favorite country to visit. I've always felt the French accent was so sexy and I've always wanted to see the Eiffel Tower, etc. And to taste the food . . . Wow.

September 2005: My uncle from England comes to meet with me in Paris at the end of the first week. We sight-see all day Saturday, then find a quaint little bistro to stop and have dinner. We were advised before we left the states to protect our wallet, the men putting them in their front pocket, instead of back pocket. So I was thinking my wallet would be safe in my pocketbook. I get up to go the restroom, with my pocketbook hanging off the back of my chair. When I get back from the restroom, my pocketbook is gone. My driver's license, credit cards, money, camera and my Mont Blanc pen (a gift from my brother) were all in that pocketbook. We report it to the police, who of course do nothing, because theft and pick-pocketing are so rampant in France. The next day is Sunday, so everything is closed and I can't get any money or credit card replacement. On Monday, I have to go to class, and then take the train back to the city to get my American Express card replaced, get money, then return to class. This whole affair has given me such a negative feeling towards France.

November 7: I have another CT scan to see how fast the cancer is spreading.

November 9: My parents drive down to Long Beach to be with me as we hear the results. God is with me and we hear "there doesn't appear to be any active cancer. It could have been an inflammation or scar tissue". The relief is indescribable and overwhelming.

December 2005: This is a very gratifying time for me. I've worked so hard for this MBA degree and am so glad my folks are able to accompany me from California to Indianapolis for the graduation ceremony. I am the first in my family to obtain a Master's and am psyched to be the first female, as well. There is snow all over the ground in Indy, which is beautiful, but caused us to be a little late for the dinner the night before the graduation. I drive as fast as I can and we are definitely the last to arrive and most people have completed their meal, the program about to begin. This is the Krannert Executive Program's ceremony. Tomorrow is the Purdue University graduation. This evening's program was quite surprising to me. Each of us is introduced and we walk to the front of the room to receive our diplomas from Krannert. When I am introduced, the Director says, "And I am extremely proud to introduce our next graduate who has overcome such great odds to be here." I was so touched, I almost started crying. Then I'm handed the diploma and continue down the faculty line shaking hands. I get to the Finance professor, who originally didn't care much for me, now gives me a great big bear hug and sincerely congratulates me. The whole thing was such an emotional time and made me so glad I made the decision to complete the program as soon as possible and to travel this far for the graduation ceremony.

The next day, I take my folks out to Ruth Chris for dinner, which is the same restaurant I took them to after my first chemo-therapy treatment in Indy. The dinner is superb. That evening, there is an ice storm, so the next morning I'm out there scraping ice off the windshield so we can get to the airport. I remember my poor little Reynaud's' fingers were so painful, I wanted to cry. It took hours for them to thaw out and stop hurting.

August 31, 2008: For some reason I dug out this journal and re-read it and felt the need to document that I've been cancer-free for three and a half years now. Three more scans and I'll be "cured". I don't know why I've been spared but I am eternally grateful.

I've been raised in the Episcopal religion all my life and have had some amount of faith throughout my life. I prayed during this entire process, but truly didn't appreciate the meaning and power of God. I just knew that this was something I had to endure and God would get me through it.

May 11, 2009: Last week I had my final CT/PET scan. Today Dr. Blitzer congratulates me on being a cancer survivor. He is my new oncologist since I moved to Long Beach, CA. He did a great job becoming familiar with my circumstances, but I wish I had Dr. Logie here to celebrate my recovery. I am no longer in remission and I no longer have any trace of active cancer. I cried. Then I brought a bottle of champagne and glasses over to my neighbors, Michael and Diane, and we had a celebratory drink.

I wish I knew why I was spared. I was given less than 1% chance of survival (okay, so here's another random statistic). My oncologists stressed that the treatments would have to be severe so I know that was a large part of the survival. Also, I maintained a positive attitude throughout the treatments. And prayer . . .

I don't focus on dying, but focus on living. Cindy has had cancer for years and is still surviving and active every day. Some days are good, others not so much, but she continues to push through it and focus on living.

December 2010: I retire from an aerospace company after thirty long years. I had another CT/PET scan to ensure I'm still cancer free. And yup I am. Six long years. I sell my Long Beach home and move to my little hometown of Atwater. Another new beginning.

COMIC RELIEF:

An old Italian man lived alone in the country. He wanted to dig his tomato garden, but it was very hard work as the ground was hard. His only son, Andres, who used to help him, was in prison. The old man wrote a letter to his son and described his predicament.

Dear Andres

I am feeling pretty bad because it looks like I won't be able to plant my tomato garden this year. I'm just getting too old to be digging up a garden plot. If you were here my troubles would be over. I know you would dig the plot for me.

Love Dad

A few days later he received a letter from his son.

Dear Dad,

Not for nothing, but don't dig up that garden. That's where I buried the BODIES.

Love Andy

At 4 a.m. the next morning, FBI agents and local police arrived and dug up the entire area without finding any bodies. They apologized to the old man and left. That same day the old man received another letter from his son.

Dear Dad,

Go ahead and plant the tomatoes now. That's the best I could do under the circumstances.

Love Andy

CHAPTER 19

Where She is Today

OCTOBER 2011: I am invited to the Atwater Relay for Life, the celebration of cancer survivors and fund raisers for Cancer Research, mostly because my childhood friend Cathy knows of my cancer history. Also she lost both parents to cancer and now has a brother who is battling cancer. I arrive and am told to park in the "cancer survivors" parking lot, then am directed to the survivors table. I'm given a T shirt and various other trinkets. I arrive there in time to make the first walk around the track. Then that night, I feel compelled to return and help people light the luminaries. Then I go back then next morning to make the final walk around the track with the survivors, then help them to pick up the luminaries. It was very moving and tearful for me, bringing back such heartfelt emotions. During the closing ceremonies several people gave testimonials, but one in particular hit me hard. One young girl got up with her mother and explained how her mother was diagnosed with cancer 11 years ago, was treated, then went another two years, was diagnosed again, treated, then diagnosed again. That was nine years ago. I thought after five years you are cured? But you know what? It's all about prayer, believing in Christ, being positive, and having a long term goal. It was about seeing my granddaughter growing up, becoming a great cook/chef, discovering what my retirement activities should be (working at the hospital, devoting my time to the church, helping the children in the community, and staying physically active, etc.).

If you have cancer or know someone who has cancer, please, please introduce them to Nadine Strain's poem "I'd Pick More Daisies", from which I've selected a few lines so you get the idea. Actually, heck, this applies to everyone, whether cancer-stricken or healthy because you just never know when or if you might contract a disease or be injured and then regret being so rigid with your life. Please note if you research this poem to read it in entirety, the poem was originally published misspelling Nadine's last name as Stair, instead of Strain. I find it awesome that she published this at the age of 85, so that we can read it today and take head sooner in life. Nadine passed in 1988, three years after this poem was published in Reader's Digest.

I'd Pick More Daisies
By Nadine Strain, age 85

If I had my life to live over,
    I'd try to make more mistakes next time.
    I would relax. I would limber up.

        I'd pick more daisies!

I knew my golden retriever, Scottey, would be perfect for pet therapy, but I didn't have the time needed to devote to this activity while I was working. Now that I'm retired, I have finally found the time to have him certified at the Share-A-Pet Foundation. He had to pass 13 tests to be certified. Goldens are bred to please, so they will naturally do anything you tell them to do, which Scottey would normally do; however he has a propensity for diarrhea when he travels. And I have a fear of heights. So travelling to San Francisco for the certification test forced us to travel twice as long as required. We couldn't go over the bridge because of its height and had to travel below San Francisco to get there. My mom volunteered to come with us, but she had to sit in the back seat because Scottey can only get into the front seat. We had to stop every 20 minutes or so, so Scottey could get out and go poop. And of course it was raining the whole way.

In the truck he didn't have room to lie down and really couldn't get in the back seat because the car opening wasn't large enough for him, so he sat up on the front seat the entire three hours it took us to get to San Francisco. Normally, a two hour trip.

When we got there, the first test was to sit. And guess what, he refused! No kidding after three hours of sitting! However, it was apparent through the rest of the tests that he is a very gentle, tentative dog and would make an excellent Pet Therapy Dog. That day was full of rain, then sun, then rain, then sun. By the time we got there, my hair was atrocious but by now you know I've lived through worse! And poor Scottey was just exhausted and dehydrated. Of course, in the end he gets certified and he spends the next year and a half absolutely making patients feel so good to pet an animal while they are stuck in the hospital. Most of them have their own pets at home that they miss terribly.

This has been one of the most rewarding things I have ever done. Since I started doing this pet therapy, there has not been a single time when someone hasn't sincerely said to me "thank you for doing this, it has meant so much to me". Some patients, as well as myself, have been moved to tears.

Scottey (Sir Scott of Lindsey, AKC) is the most humble, gentle, tentative dogs I've had the gratitude of living with. I bought him when he was two months old and he was so much fun. He ran with me every day until we both got too old and got too many ailments to keep doing that. Then we walked every day, about two miles. Now he can no longer go for walks. He has arthritis, is deaf, is losing his sight, has kidney disease, but still tries to jump up and down for his food. And because he can't hear, he imagines he hears things and will bark at nothing. Still providing enjoyment and pleasure!

Unfortunately he passed in May of 2013. I cried off and on for two weeks.

Then I decided to start fostering rescue pets. I contacted Tech-for-Pets, a wonderful non-profit here in Atwater (who could use any donations you might want to offer!) and let them know I'm ready to be a foster parent. The first pet they gave me was Mr. Franklin, (Frankie) a two year old cat, whose tail had to be amputated. But that hasn't prevented him from jumping anywhere he wants to. The first day he arrived at my home, he did not eat anything for 24 hours and that worried me. But then by noon the next day he started eating. Now he rules the roost and has a pension for knocking expensive things off the counters. Cheap things are irrelevant. I adopted him within about six months.

September 2013: I finally feel able to bring another golden retriever into my home. From the Northern California Golden Retriever Rescue Organization, I have now acquired an 11 year old named Hannah. She was given up by her family due to excessive medical requirements. The Nor Cal Rescue Org paid for her surgeries and Cushing's tests, then called and asked if I would like to adopt her. I went to Sacramento to meet her and immediately fell in love. She had a patch of fur missing from her back as a result of the Cushing's Disease and she was about 20 pounds overweight.

Today, thanks to the Vetyrol she takes daily, her fur has grown back, she has shed the excess weight, she gets along well with my two rescue cats and she has been working at the hospital every Friday as a pet therapy dog, just like Scottey did.

On Sunday, we are in church and the priest asks for people to stand up and talk about what they are most grateful for. Blowing me away, my dad stands up (remember the not-so-demonstrative guy I mentioned earlier?) and talks about how grateful he is to have my mother as his wife. Then my mother, who also is not a comfortable public speaker, jumps up and states how happy she is that

I have survived aggressive cancer and am serving in the church. See how God works? Not only did he save me, but he made my folks more out-going to speak of Christ and how he works in our lives.

Then the attention turns to me and I feel compelled to talk about a conference I was somewhat forced to attend for Love INC (Love, In the Name of Christ). Love INC provides donations of all kinds to persons in need in the community. During the process of giving, we try to encourage those in need to seek Christ in their lives. I really didn't want to go to the conference . . . it was in Illinois and I am so tired of travelling. I did so much of that with my job. But I reluctantly go and there was a lady who spoke on the first day about peeling away the layers of our heart that are extraneous to our lives . . . vanity, reputation, greed, anger, anxiety, selfishness etc. This is a life-long commitment to Christ. Then the second day, she told us to put down our pencils and just listen (of course, having heard her powerful talk the previous day I knew I couldn't not take notes; she was so awesome and I knew I would never remember everything I needed to hear) so I stood in the back of the room and took notes. She then spoke about re-building our hearts with the Christ-like actions such as love, compassion, encouragement, hope, patience, humility, and grace that make us the Christians God expects of us. There was something so truly humble and unassuming about her that I remember her talk to this day and strive to become more like that attitude. I made it a point to approach her after her talk on the second day to tell her how impressed I was with her talk and she kind of looked at me like "don't praise me, I was only sharing God's message!" And that told me to learn about humility.

October 2013: I got a call from Techs for Pets and they have six kittens and a momma that they rescued from a trailer in Merced. So, of course I had to go see them and ended up picking a solid black kitten, naming him Zephyr. Being territorial, Frankie did not accept Zephyr for quite a while. He stayed in my closet for two days, not eating or peeing. Then he moved to an extra bedroom for a couple of days, then slowly came out and introduced himself to the new kitty. There were times when Frankie would jump up on my bed at night expecting to sleep there, and then realize Zephyr was there and Frankie would hiss and shriek, then jump off the bed. Poor Frankie. They're such funny creatures.

November 2013: Now Frankie and Zephyr play together and are best buds!

My sister, Liz, used to ask me when I was stressed about something at work, a problem with a neighbor, the house maintenance, money problems, etc . . . "Is it a ten?" In other words is the problem I'm worrying about the most important thing in your life that you need to stress about it? Cancer may be a ten, but remember to put the rest of your life into perspective as well.

As I've mentioned, I've struggled with "why did I survive"? What does God want from me? I retired in December 2010 from an aerospace company after thirty years. I bought and moved into my dream home and have immersed myself into Community Service. I am actively involved in my church and I'm the VP/CFO of a non-profit foundation called Happy Feet, which is a federally certified, non-profit organization created by Brynn Wolcott (this foundation also would appreciate any donations you might want to make!). We provide new shoes for needy children in the community and have had two totally moving and rewarding donations over the past two years.

January 2014: I was asked to bring Hannah to the Cancer Clinic for their monthly support group sessions. How ironic is that, that the oncologist doctor would ask me to bring my dog to the Cancer Support Group, without knowing that I, myself, am also a cancer survivor?? We attend each month, but in March 2014, there is a cancer exercise specialist who speaks to the group. Her name is Starr Carson Cleary and she speaks of the benefits of exercise and most importantly breathing from the core which reminds me of how poorly I've been breathing since my treatments and also how so DOWN on the couch I was for so long during my treatments, which probably caused some muscle atrophy. What I would have given for her expertise when I was able to get back up and do my walking, then running every day! This is a fairly new (last ten years) regime that is proving helpful to recovering cancer patients. I asked her if this was nationwide and she indicated no, not yet. But if you're interested, the practice is called "Regenerations, Wellness Cancer Foundation". One of her patients who attended her sessions swears by her methods and says she doesn't want to stop attending.

2014: Since the beginning of this journey, I have had about 18 CT and/or PET scans, an MRI, countless blood draws, five surgeries, two hospital stays, weekly chemo for six months, simultaneously with 33 days of radiation. It had a toll of my body which took about 18 months to recover from; however, this is 2014 and I am celebrating my tenth year being cancer free!

I have continually asked myself and God why He has spared me. I attended a Bible Study group from my church which studied the book, "The Purpose Driven Life: What on Earth Am I Here For". Initially I was convinced the book would provide me with the reason why I was spared. I came to understand there would be no lightning bolt to strike me on the head and tell me why I was spared. It is instead to be a learning experience, a slow process of accepting God, peeling away the layers of those unnecessary things such as reputation, greed, impatience, pride, gloating, etc., then renewing the heart, mind, body and soul with the really true things we need in our lives: patience, love, compassion, giving, prayer, community service, and family.

And to bring it around full circle, I still have Reynaud's in my index fingers, hurting so much in the winter when it's cold and not so much in the summer.

I've taken up golf, have caught the bug and am going to the range as often as I can. It's a frustrating game of contorting your body to perfectly swing a long stick at a small ball! It's humbling, yet frustrating.

I still work out every day for about an hour. Then several days each week, I play tennis for about an hour. Interestingly enough, I can't run or jog for more than a block or so without having to stop and catch my breath so I guess the neuropathy will continue for the rest of my life.

My oncologists told me in the beginning that they would have to hit me hard with the treatments and they did, but they saved my life. I am forever grateful to them for that. Every July (the month I was diagnosed) I send Dr. Logie a thank-you note telling him that I am still kicking and letting him know what's going on in my life and that I am so grateful to him.

So, if you're reading this (well, of course, you're reading this, otherwise, you wouldn't be reading this!) and are facing a cancer diagnosis (or know someone who is), how will you attack this monster? What goals will you establish? How positive can you be during your journey? Do you have a support system to rely on? If not, contact me. I want to give back and be there for you. This is terrifying for you and you may need someone to talk to. I can say that I've been there. Also, there are many, many services available to you at no cost, so do the research whenever you need something or a professional to help you.

There is a quote engraved on the entrance to the hospital that I volunteer for which states "Every person is a gift and every life is a blessing". You are that gift and that blessing!

God Bless you,
Susan Nix

CHRISTIAN RELIEF:

Two traveling angels stopped to spend the night in the home of a wealthy family. The family was rude and refused to let the angels stay in the mansion's guest room. Instead the angels were given a small space in the cold basement. As they made their bed on the hard floor, the older angel saw a hole in the wall and repaired it. When the younger angel asked why, the older angel replied, "Things aren't always what they seem".

The next night the pair came to rest at the house of a very poor, but very hospitable farmer and his wife. After sharing what little food they had the couple let the angels sleep in their bed where they could have a good night's rest. When the sun came up the next morning the angels found the farmer and his wife in tears. Their only cow, whose milk had been their sole income, lay dead in the field. The younger angel was infuriated and asked the older angel how could you have let this happen? The first man had everything, yet you helped him, she accused. The second family had little but was willing to share everything, and you let the cow die. "Things aren't always what they seem," the older angel replied. "When we stayed in the basement of the mansion, I noticed there was gold stored in that hole in the wall. Since the owner was so obsessed with greed and unwilling to share his good fortune, I sealed the wall so he wouldn't find it." "Then last night as we slept in the farmers bed, the angel of death came for his wife I gave him the cow instead. Things aren't always what they seem." Sometimes that is exactly what happens when things don't turn out the way they should. If you have faith, you just need to trust that every outcome is always as it should be: God's will.

Printed in Great Britain
by Amazon